Escape: Rehab Your Brain to Stay Out of the Legal System

Escape: Rehab Your Brain to Stay Out of the Legal System

Written By Dr. Jay Faber

Edited by Thomas P. Smith

ISBN-13: 9781541026629
ISBN-10: 1541026624
Library of Congress Control Number: 2016920575
CreateSpace Independent Publishing Platform
North Charleston, South Carolina

Legal & Disclaimer

Table of Contents

Preface

Over the past decade, there has been an increasing belief that innovation in the United States is at a standstill. The glowing years of new groundbreaking products, services, and technology have not kept up with the pace of yesteryear. Subsequently, a deadening mindset that this country is losing some of its edge with promising research and development has emerged. Maybe America is not the great land of possibility where a hard work ethic and an iron-fisted belief in a new idea can make the world a better place.

Although this festering viewpoint has gained traction, there is at least one individual who appears to be demonstrating that this is a pessimistic, indeed, wrong approach...His name is Elon Musk.

South African-born Elon Musk moved to the United States in 1992, obtaining degrees in both economics and physics at the University of Pennsylvania. After graduating, Musk moved to California to attend Stanford's PhD physics program. Only two days after beginning his studies, Musk quit. He decided to pursue his entrepreneurial dreams in renewable energy, space exploration, and the Internet.

His decision proved to be a profitable one. Musk became recognized for his start-up company, PayPal, that eventually gave him a $180 million profit sale.[1] Although he received a highly lucrative return, one of his more current endeavors may prove even more profitable and make the world a better place to live.

In 2003, Musk cofounded a new company, Tesla Motors. The primary purpose of the company was to make a sleek, gliding, aesthetically pleasing, fast electric car that motorists would salivate to own. Musk did not start this company for financial gain.[2] Instead, his burning motivation was fueled to produce a vehicle that ran just as fast as current cars, but would not leave a biological footprint of toxic fumes within the environment.

The heart and soul of this titanium "Formula One like" creation can be found under its strong supportive main frame. Not visible from its exterior, there lies an estimated 1,200 pound, 112 inches by 77 inches foot electric battery that powers this vehicle to speeds up to 155 mph. Moreover, this voltaic source will travel 270 miles before it needs to be recharged.3

There is one other proposition that makes the Tesla even more enticing. This incentive could revolutionize transportation in the 21st century. For those who decide to buy a Tesla, Musk has begun to create "Supercharge Stations" for its customers. Rather than plugging in your car at home, an owner can go to a station, plug in their car, wait only 20 minutes, and your car is ready to go...efficient, fast, and easy!

Oh, there is one other minor glitch that should be mentioned. While gas consumers are forking out over $3 per gallon at their local Chevron and QT stations, how much do you think the Tesla owner will be paying at the Supercharge Stations per refill? Thirty dollars? Twenty Dollars? Ten Dollars? Five Dollars? No! The Tesla owners will pay absolutely nothing...zippo; the charge is F-R-E-E! Yes, I was not serious about that notion of a minor glitch.

How broad and expansive will these stations be in terms of economy of scale? Today, if you purchased a car in Los Angeles you could actually drive your car to New York City and not pay one single dime for energy.4 Supercharge stations have been strategically placed to ensure that no car is "left behind" without a charge.

The story gets even better. There are numerous Superstations popping up now all over the country. Moreover, Musk is now working to have the Superstations use solar energy to produce the electricity. It's wild to think of the prospect of pure clean energy with no biological bruises to the environment!

As this story continues to unfold, it may very well be one of the most inspirational stories of the 21st century. Musk could very well be the next Andrew Carnegie, Jack Welch, Steve Jobs, or Richard Branson who makes a profound difference that radicalizes how energy is produced.

As the "Do you believe in miracles?" Tesla vehicles and Supercharge Stations begin to permeate our society, there is yet another product that may prove to be even more valuable. As technologies advance, this biological wonder will also be writing its own story over the next several decades. It creates, inspires, and imagines. It makes us laugh, cry, and wonder. It celebrates, endures, and moves us forward. What is more interesting is that each of you will be very much a part of this journey, because you already personally own one.

So what exactly is this "Microsoft-like" gadgetry? The priceless bio-electronic instrument is your brain. Your brain sees, hears, smells, and feels. It helps us walk, run, skip, and glide. It helps us think, analyze, assess, and create.

When our brain works well, we are in better physical health, think more clearly, feel more vividly, and produce more effectively. We are bolder, more persistent, and mentally tenacious. We are more likely to inspire, transform, and make the world a better place to live.

Yet, when our brains aren't working so well, all sorts of dire consequences can occur. In such situations, we are more likely to be complacent, nervous, and depressed. Our energy will be lower, our motivation will be lackluster, and our belief in ourselves will be duller. We become more passive, lacking focus, not pursuing desire.

Just as Musk has dug deeply to understand how the power of the battery can transform modern culture, the field of neuroscience has developed new technologies to better grasp how our brain works. Most exciting, this new knowledge has started to teach us how to better take care of our brains and more fully ignite its silent power.

This book has been devoted to a specific group of individuals who could highly benefit from neuroscience. That stigmatized entity are those people who have been actively involved in the legal systems: criminals, felons, convicts, thieves, murderers, crooks, prisoners, frauds, and other pejorative connotations.

These labels can bring up instant associations with Al Capone, Jesse James, Charles Manson, Ted Bundy, Bonnie and Clyde, Eric Rudolph, and the Unabomber. These are the "bad guys," the "outlaws," the "evil ones," and the "misfits" of society.

As you will learn in this book, neuroscience is beginning to find out that not all these indecent souls are just "lock them up and throw the key away" pariahs. They are not bad people. Instead, they have bad brains, and those bad brains are leading to bad decisions, and those bad decisions are leading to bad behaviors, and those bad behaviors are leading to getting a "go directly to jail" card.

The purpose of this book is to harness what we have learned (so far) in neuroscience to help rehabilitate these poorly functioning brains and create more positively contributing citizens to society. Rather than living a life in a sequestered 8 feet by 8 feet jail cell or hibernating in a dilapidated parolee group home, we now might actually be able to make a difference. What if were able to transform these negatively labeled "low-lifes" into fulfilled, hard-working, contributing members of society?

Not only would the plagued individual reap the benefits of such research advances, so, too would all the responsible tax-paying citizens. What if we truly were able to create a system that cut the number of inmates in the legal system by 50 percent? What if we were able to find constructive ways to keep those convicted of a crime from ever returning to a prison ever again? What would this do to our states' budgets? Better yet, what would it do to our country's gargantuan budget deficit? From a personal perspective, what would it do to your annual income tax return?

Does this sound crazy? Does this sound improbable? Does this sound like a good time to ingest a couple of our "cable news networks' attitude of skepticism" capsules? (I know some will) Neuroscience prefers to remain a bit more resilient, similar to Musk. We believe that we can take our cold, scientifically analyzed "factoids" and create a better world for all.

How personally convinced am I of this endeavor? Many told me that I was crazy to write it, because no one would purchase it; it would only serve a small economic market and would not bring home the profit margin needed to be a financial success.

Believe it or not, the purpose of this book was not to reap financial gain and a more lucrative lifestyle (I have future ideas of that for a later time). Instead, the sole purpose of this book is to reveal the possibility of what neuroscience can do to develop a stronger and vibrant society by getting our brains to a more healthy level of functioning. I hope that all will take heart and practically apply what is written in the following pages. Moreover, I hope that this will be a stepping stone for bigger and better things to come. The written material is not an "end all" and "be all" pontification of how to rehabilitate the criminal mind. I hope that others will constructively read, analyze, and critique it so that future ideas are even more productive.

In closing, I have personally dedicated this book to the Federal and State governments of the United States of America. Although we all, including myself, can find lots to complain about, I am very grateful for this country. Financially, I would not have been able to attend medical school without the assistance of government-subsidized loans. This book is a brief synopsis of some of what I have learned from those loans. May it be used to make this country and world a better place.

A printed copy of this book is for sale online at Amazon.com and additional copies - you need to print on your own- are available at www.drjayfaber.com

Introduction

Eric's mother forced her son to come to our office to have a psychiatric evaluation. After being placed on numerous emotional assessments, several trips to drug rehabilitation facilities, and bi-monthly trips to the local county jail, Eric's mother was fed up. She was frustrated, concerned, and worn out.

In contrast, Eric's attitude reflected minimal desire to change. Drugs were the only vehicle that gave him some solemn relief from his internal anguish. He had earnestly tried to feel better by taking constructive, non-addictive measures. They just weren't helping.

Stealing, selling drugs, using illicit substances, and manipulating the family combined with a "dash" of temper tantrums and a "slice" of physical fights were Eric's daily sustenance, his outline for "how to live life"...until he came to our office.

When I first met Eric, his attitude permeated with cynicism, doubt, and disgust for my profession. And who could blame Eric? Let's face the facts. He had already been to several psychiatrists, placed on dozens of medications, and spent thousands of dollars with minimal, if any success. Now, his mother was going to spend several more thousand dollars...on functional neuroimaging, a procedure that would take three whole days to complete? This is going to make a difference? Really?

Despite all the negativity, Eric proceeded and went through the evaluation. At the end of the assessment, Eric, his mother, and I discussed our neurophysiological findings and came up with a tentative plan to help his brain function at a better level.

Over the initial months, Eric was highly challenged. He was hospitalized twice having thoughts of wanting to harm himself. There was a point when Eric was asked to leave his family's home. Subsequently, he went to live with friends who were using illicit substances. Finally, Eric had spent most of his money irresponsibly, resulting in his entering a group home.

During this "rocky road" start, Eric, his mother, his stepfather, and I did not give up. Several nights a week, I would get phone calls from his mother and stepfather about what else they could do. Between these communications, I would telephone Eric. Sometimes, he would speak; other times he would be elusive. Sometimes he would be open and honest; at other times, he would be outright deceptive. Sometimes, Eric would be sincere about wanting to change; at other times, he would suddenly shift to trickery and lies.

Eric was difficult. Eric was manipulative. Eric was exhausting. But... all parties were personally committed not to give up. We fought for Eric even when he did not feel like fighting for himself. His exhausted mother would come up with new schemes that would hopefully be different than past endeavors. His emotionally drained stepfather would personally take Eric to all of his appointments even though he fought "tooth and nail" all the way.

Somewhere in this process, Eric began to change. Following his placement in a group home, there were beginning signs of more positive daily habits. At the group home, a very tight structure and regimented scheduling became a focused part of his lifestyle. In addition, angry, manipulative outbursts would no longer be tolerated. Disagreements were encouraged; but there could not be any name-calling, yelling, or physical destruction. Rules could be challenged, but they always had to be followed. Discipline, commitment, accountability, integrity, and follow-through became the "new norm" at the group home.

During his office visits, Eric started demonstrating more control over his volatile temper. Through the use of supplements, medication, and therapy, Eric began to understand what prompted him to become so frustrated. Moreover, he developed new skill sets to de-intensify his unpleasant feelings. Finally, he started to take accountability, personally owning his brain's neurophysiology, so that he could make even more positive changes.

Over the past year and a half, Eric has not been back to jail. (He had been going approximately every two months.) Eric has remained sober. Eric has found constructive ways to express his anger. Eric has since gone back to school. He was accepted at a music school and has been actively pursuing a degree in music production. Eric now has hopes. Eric now has dreams. Eric now has a life.

The purpose of this workbook is to help others who have personally been involved with the legal system stay out of it...forever! For those of you who have been in jail, placed on probation, given early release on parole, or are currently in prison, this is a book to help you demand more out of yourself and to reach goals you never thought possible, just like Eric.

How likely will you stay out of the legal system?

When looking at Eric's case, he is one of the more fortunate ones. In reality, the majority of those individuals who have been in prison or jail will return back to that system. Only 40 percent of those who are released from jail/prison will successfully complete their parole requirements (From: http://www.bjs.gov/content/reentry/success.cfm). That means that more than half of those prisoners released will end up back in the very same place to which they never wanted to return.

Hard, cold, and sobering as these harsh numbers appear, it is reality. This is the unpleasant truth. The majority of prisoners will end up in the same place they never wanted to set foot in ever again. Why does this happen? How do we make sense of this phenomenon? What is the emotional, social, and economic cost to society?

To make matters even more complicated, there is another important facet to add to this sinister web. As successful as Eric has been so far in his release from the legal system, the likelihood of him staying out will depend on his daily, methodical, and rigorous practice of the skill sets that he has been learning. If he starts to take shortcuts, minimize their importance, or rationalize not doing the daily, necessary, fundamental behaviors, he will most likely end up back in the system.

What Do You Need to Bring to Make This Journey Work?

Given these somber facts, there are new technologies emerging to help manage this dilemma. Throughout the pages of this workbook, you will be trained and expected to live up to goals that you never dreamed possible. For those of you who think this will be "just" another unsuccessful combination of "psycho" techniques to get you to change, then that is what the system will be. As Henry Ford so simply stated, "Whether you think you can or you think you can't--you're right." The system cannot change your beliefs. Only you have the fortitude within yourself to make that choice.

Should you embark on this journey, here are some initial internal attributes you will need to carry to take with you. First, you are going to need to learn to develop a high tolerance for failure. The reality is that you will make many mistakes. More often than not, you will fall flat on your face. The reality is that you won't feel comfortable.

You won't die. You won't feel harsh physical pain. You won't be risking any limbs. You simply will experience discomfort. This internal disorientation is not meant to be punishing. Instead, it is a sign that your decision to change is leading you to master new, more constructive behaviors. These initial "first steps" will need some "tweaking" to get moving in the right direction. But, it is the fact that you are moving, trying something new, and experimenting with constructive novelty that are good signs.

Secondly, it will be imperative that you begin to develop an increased willingness to learn. This desire means that you earnestly want to find life-giving answers to your daily problems. "What can I do to find a better paying job?" "How can I find a more stable living situation?" "I know that I need to find better friends, but where do I go to do that?"

The questions asked can be relatively simple. However, if left unanswered, they can potentially lead you back to where you started--back in jail or prison. Instead of recreating that scenario, I encourage you to try to put the jigsaw puzzle together and tolerate the discomfort. This uneasiness often stops many from finding unknown answers. Please do not let it paralyze you.

You are going to need to develop skill sets to teach you how to learn. You are going to need skill sets to manage your brain when you feel the malaise on the journey. You are going to need to believe that the end of the road can and will bring forth great satisfaction.

In order to learn, you will need to bring along some new "best friends" as quoted by Rudyard Kipling.

Developing a willingness to learn means asking questions with these "six serving comrades"! Notably, bang on their doors when you are tired, frustrated, ready to quit, and fatigued. That is when you will need them the most. If you keep them close, they will serve, guide, instruct, forebear, pursue, and push you to new, challenging limits.

So, as we become more aware of how to become better learners, we have to cultivate a positive internal culture that moves you forward on your journey. Let's face the facts: life is not easy. It is difficult. It is hard. It offers a minimal number of winning lottery tickets

For those of you in the legal system, it is often more problematic. Many come from poor socioeconomic conditions. Many have not had stable caregivers in childhood. Many have not had great experiences in school. The sum of those life situations painfully engrave a number of self-limiting, destructive beliefs.

Even more concerning, many are not aware of these unconscious limitations within. They fester. They stagnate. They rust. They are the mildew that decay and limit lifestyle changes.

Creating a positive internal culture means that we must become more aware of those hostile, terroristic beliefs and develop our own "homeland security" to attack them. Our internal system replaces those invasive intruders with stronger, more resilient, and mentally tough affirmative statements.

This work is not for the weary. Many strong men and women will not have the fortitude to address these strongholds on their life. Furthermore, even if they do have the heart to look at their decomposing corrosion, will they have the persistent, tenacious fight to beat them? The internal battle may not make the best script for a Hollywood A-list movie. But, the intensity needed to counterattack is just, if not more, intense than any blockbuster action-packed saga.

Creating a positive internal culture may seem soft. It may seem overly simplistic. It may seem like adding a sugar coating. Don't be fooled. This is going to be a battle. It is going to be demanding. It will push you just as hard as any armed services recruit going through basic training.If you take this endeavor lightly, you will lose--that I can guarantee. There is nothing more satisfying to your negative, entrenched beliefs than to look at yourself square in the face and laughingly say, "See, I told you so, how stupid are you to think you could change?"

So my advice is: please don't take the notion of affirming beliefs lighthearted. Don't be naive. Be strong. Be courageous. Be a confronter, and create a more positive internal culture.

Finally, you are going to need to develop trust in this process and trust in the people who are trying to help you move forward. For many, this will be the most challenging process. Trust flourishes when we believe that we are being heard, when our perceptions are accepted, and when our needs are valued.

This concept will be much different than the experiences you are about to encounter with your mentors. Specifically, many of your behaviors, beliefs, and attitudes will not be accepted, and your supervisor will be expecting you to change, not just be understood. Subsequently, you could perceive your supervisor (or the system) as being unfair, cruel, and working against you (i.e.-there is no trust!). Because of this chasm, you are going to be more vulnerable to angrily act out, go against what is suggested, and risk being sent back to jail.

Before acting out in such a risky manner, contemplate on what else might be happening. Your personal beliefs, perceptions, attitudes, and behaviors have unfortunately led you into the valley of trouble. Problems with self-esteem, chaotic families, and unstable relationships have resulted in where you are today.

Your supervisor (and the system) is well aware that your brain patterns are going to need to change in order for you to stay out of the penal system. He/she is going to be confronting your negative self-perceptions, demanding that you don't think so little of yourself, and commanding you to take accountability for the lifestyle you are creating. Inconsistent stories will be probed. Withholding information will be censored. Deceptive tactics will be queried.

In this type of parolee-supervisor relation, where does trust come in? Where is the empathy? Where is the encouragement? Where is the understanding? Where is the unconditional acceptance?

Trust is never freely given...to any of us. You are going to have to earn it by demonstrating honest, consistent, and earnest behavior. This is not easy. This is hard. Your brain and emotional state are not going to like it...at all!

This challenge gets further complicated by the childhood attachments you may have experienced with your caregivers. Research indicates that about 60 percent of individuals have grown up in homes where there were secure attachments. In this environment, caregivers tend to react quickly to meet the needs of their children. They are attuned with their emotions, engage interactively with them, and make sure that their environment is safe. The children of these surroundings are typically less aggressive, less oppositional, and more in control of their emotions.

As these children mature into adulthood, they become more trusting and able to have mature relationships.

In addition, they are more aware of their own internal states, can comfortably identify their needs, and find constructive ways to meet them. (http://psychology.about.com/od/loveandattraction/ss/attachmentstyle_4.htm; About.com; Attachment styles, by Kendra Cherry)

In contrast, 40 percent of children grow up where caregivers are not as nurturing. In these homes, parental figures are not consistent in caring, dismissive of acknowledging important child needs, and lack the ability to be aware of their toddler's emotional states. Such rearing leads to insecure attachments.

In this scenario, children often don't feel safe and lack awareness of their emotional needs. Consequently, they struggle to control their anger, connect with others, and follow rules. They are often labeled as troubled children, disrespectful, and not likely to succeed.

As they mature into adults, the earlier predictions often become true. The social misfits can't hold jobs, they can't develop quality relationships, and most importantly, they can't trust others. To cope, many of these insecure attached adults turn to drugs and alcohol to meet their nurturing needs. They lack empathy. They steal. They lie. They end up in jails and prisons.

This mixture of being lovingly challenged and growing up with insecure homes has all the ingredients of a combustible concoction leading to anger, suspicion, and doubt. If this inevitable conflict is not constructively confronted, there is a high likelihood of acting out your feelings, resulting in unwanted consequences.

Trust in people, in a system, and in a process will be essential for you to succeed. Without trust, your likelihood to succeed will go down markedly. On this journey you will experience discomfort, you will be disrupted, and you will be put at unease. Why? Because the essence of the very people and system who are guiding you are going to challenge you to change.

In reality, you know you have to change as well. You know if things are not done differently, you could end up back in jail or prison. You know that your behaviors have led you down the wrong path.

But to trust? After all the inconsistencies you experienced as a child? After all the broken promises from your caregivers? After all the lies, critical comments, and lack of encouragement?

Changing behavior is not going to be the real challenge. Learning to trust someone; acknowledging conflict constructively and resolving it; and accepting that maybe, just maybe, there are some people out there who truly care...this will be where the rubber truly hits the road. Game on...are you up to it?

What is so Different About This Program?

So as we go on this journey of trust together, some of you may consciously (and others unconsciously) ask, "Hey, there are a bunch of programs, group homes, parole officers, and government programs already out there. Why should I take the time and emotional energy, with the little amount of trust and great deal of skepticism I have, to engagingly commit to this workbook?"

First, if you were thinking this way or you started to spontaneously think, that is a great question. Why should you trust another system, one that might even let you down more than in the past? If you have been burned before, isn't it likely that this system will also lead to failure?

Most programs in the past have utilized both a psychological and social approach to help lead you down a path of constructive living. As such, many of these programs are very good and would be considered "state of the art," powerfully moving experiences.

This workbook will most likely have similar themes from past programs. However, there is one significant area where it begins to differentiate. As we embark into the 21st century, new technologies are allowing the scientific community to better understand how the human brain functions. New, advanced digital tools such as fMRI, PET scans, QEEG, and SPECT scans are opening up new frontiers to how our brains work.

One finding that is becoming increasingly clear is that individuals who end up in the legal system typically have brains that are not working so well. For example, the rate of traumatic brain injury is seven times higher in prisons and jails. Moreover, about 85 percent of prisoners have a substance abuse problem. These piercing numbers are beginning to illuminate that many prisoners are not just "bad" people. They have unhealthy brains, and society must embark on a new approach to learn how to rehabilitate them.

The essence of what is different in this workbook: this course will use the very best of psychological/social interventions to promote your success, and it will add the best of what 21st century medical science has to offer to help your brain be healthier. A healthy brain feels better, a healthy brain thinks wiser, a healthier brain demonstrates more constructive behaviors that lead to a higher quality of life.

What Life Skill Sets Are You Going to Need to Master?

Below are the skill sets that you are going to need to master to create a better lifestyle and stay out of the legal system:

- Create a Daily Schedule
- Build a Strong Network of High Quality and Sustainable Relationships
- Develop a Powerful Resilient Self-Esteem
- Stay Sober
- Develop and Grow

If you successfully learn to incorporate these five attributes into your daily lifestyle, you will do well. Their essence is simple. They are straightforward, commonsense, and pragmatic. They are not overly profound, earth-shattering breakthroughs, or lightning bolts of insight.

These skill sets are like a painting that you, the artist, are going to use to create your own masterpiece. The amount of time, energy, and dedication that you commit to this system will result in the quality of how the final rendition looks. Will your masterpiece lifestyle lead to a well-respected painting in a distinguished museum of art or, instead, will your purposeless "scribbles" be buried in the bottom of a rusting dumpster?

Before this journey starts, I would highly encourage you to contemplate and ask... are you up for this challenge? Are you willing to deal with mistakes, laugh at yourself, and remain calm as you peer into the chasm of frustration? Will you allow yourself to tolerate some discomfort, tension, and awkwardness as you experiment with more constructive behaviors? Will you be willing to encourage yourself to move forward when every bone, fiber, and muscle demand that you fall back into the "woe is me" victim role? Finally (and probably the most difficult), will you be willing to let go and trust? Will you be willing to parachute out of the plane of life, trust that your instructor has your best long-term interests at heart, and learn how to develop more healthy attachments?

Should you genuinely answer "yes" to these questions, welcome aboard. This workbook and your cast of support is ready to begin a trip that you, internally, will not forget.

At the end of each chapter, there will be a number of questions for you to answer. Rather than trying to answer all the questions, it is suggested that you only try to answer five of them. By taking such an approach, you will hopefully find yourself more engaged and less overwhemed.

Summary

This workbook can help you learn to paint your own "Renoir." But you, and only you, can choose to practice daily these four essential qualities:

- A Tolerance for Failure
- A Willingness to Learn
- Creating a Positive Internal Culture
- Developing a Trust that the System is Helping You

CHAPTER 1

Scheduling

Will was a 26-year-old male who had been living on the streets. This lifestyle was a marked contrast to that of nine years earlier. At that time, Will was getting ready to graduate from high school, get further education, and discover what he wanted to do for the rest of his life.

Those aspirations changed after Will was introduced to drugs. What started off as a fun recreational hobby turned into an out-of-control habit that became the center of his life. Morning, noon, and evening, Will became consumed with finding, purchasing, and using illicit substances.

Slowly and gradually, Will's habit seeking aspirations led to a markedly different lifestyle than that which he had planned in high school. Goal setting, hard work, and persistence were replaced with taking shortcuts, living for the moment, and leisure. These new values did not hurt anyone. He was just having fun. What's wrong with that?

In the end, Will found himself living on the streets. Without a job, a place to live, or food for nourishment, one would think that the discomfort would lead to some values clarification and behavioral change. Unfortunately, as with many substance abusers, Will had not hit "rock bottom." He was still mesmerized with finding, purchasing, and using recreational drugs. The immediate pleasure from them was just too hard to let go.

It was at this point that Will's mother reached out to me. She was concerned that it was only a matter of time before Will got himself involved in another organizational entity...the legal system. If that consequence were to occur, Will would be placed in an environment that would be far less flexible and open to suggestions.

Unwilling (and angry), Will grudgingly came to my office due to his mom's persistence. During his visit, our clinic took some functional brain imaging pictures, known as Single Photon Emission Computed Tomography (SPECT) scans. These data-driven pictures offer a firsthand look at how the brain is performing. In Will's case, his use of drugs had demonstrated some concerning findings. The scans revealed that the surface of his brain, which is normally smooth from good blood flow, had numerous bumps, holes, and scalloping. These unsightly findings are indicative of a toxic brain, a brain that has been severely traumatized from the use of harmful drugs.

Reflecting on his pictures, Will began to ponder on how his brain had been affected by his destructive behaviors. He was rather aghast at the findings. His antagonism and doubt were beginning to wilt, not completely, but they were starting to bend. Subsequently, Will made a decision that he would try to work on a brain-health strategy for at least a month. The door was opened...and I took full advantage to start to develop a proactive brain-health plan with Will.

During that discussion, I mentioned to Will that there would be one behavior that he would need to do if we were going to move forward. This behavior was not to start taking psychotropic medication to alleviate cravings. (After all, I am a psychiatrist. Is that not what we typically recommend?)

The behavior was not to start taking vitamins and supplements to initiate health brain functioning. Medically, is this not one of the top priorities that should be started to create an optimal biological environment?

The initial most important behavior was not even to stop taking drugs and alcohol. What? Will was even shocked at this point. (Please note also that I am trying to develop buy-in and create a therapeutic environment.) Will was expecting me to be another "command from above authority figure," to lay down the law and say, "You have to stop doing drugs." Instead, he was being asked intriguing questions that would lead to buy-in, curiosity, and more engagement.

So if these behaviors were not the most important, what, in heaven's sake, was Will supposed to do? Please note that by this time, I had created enough tension and inquisitiveness to get Will's full, undivided attention. "Will, here is the first thing that you must do...You simply need to sit down and create a daily schedule."

I did not have to wait long for the resistance to start. "What? A schedule," he cynically commented, "I don't like them. I don't even own a calendar. I can't even afford to buy one. What am I supposed to use to create a schedule? Am I supposed to use my food money to get one? Further, this sounds really tedious. Do I have to fill every hour of the day with menial tasks? This makes no sense to me...at all!"

Having been through the barrage of excuses, reasoning, and reprimands before, I smiled back at Will and said, "I agree with you. We are going to make this cheap (like "0 dollars"), and we aren't going to make this a complicated endeavor. All you need to do is break your day up into thirds: morning, noon, and night, and just do one constructive activity in each of those time periods. All you need to do is one activity every four hours."

I gave Will some examples to help. I mentioned that he might want to go work out in the morning to rejuvenate his physical health. In the afternoon, Will could attend a support group to find new friends to encourage sobriety (and health for his brain). During the evening, he could go to a movie, hang out at a bookstore, or watch an educational show on the Web.

Understandably doubting me, I challenged Will. "Just give it a week," I commented, "What do you have to lose? There is not a job or other responsibility you have to do during this time. Have some fun with it, and report back to me in one week."

We will come back and share more of Will's escapades. It gets really interesting.

A Schedule? Really?

As this topic is brought up, there may be long sighs and pessimistic dislikes of having to do such a mundane task. Creating a schedule makes you feel like you are a student in school (again), not an educated adult. The very thought goes against the grain of freedom and being freely able to do what one wants. It may seem restricting. It may seem inhibiting. It may be seen as some type of manipulative game an authoritative adult is trying to use to just fill up excess time.

To add even more fuel, any type of schedule will involve change. The essence of change is hard and typically not pleasurable. Some old habits will cease. Some pleasurable activities will go away and will be replaced by other constructive events. Will these new behaviors replace some of your past enjoyments or will I walk away empty-handed, shortchanged, and, "screwed" for creating a schedule?

It's not only a change in behaviors that will need to occur. Our personal beliefs about a schedule may need transformation. "A schedule? This is going to be way too hard." "If I put something on my schedule, then I will be forced to do it." "I could not control myself before; is a schedule really going to make that big of a difference?" "Once I get frustrated, I won't follow a schedule. I will just go back to my old ways." "I have never done a schedule. I don't even know what that means."

A Quick Lesson on Our Brains

Neuroscience is beginning to discover that our brains have a particular way of functioning when in an "autopilot" state. We call this state our Default Mode Network. Our Default Mode Network is like a personal fingerprint. We each have our own way of being in "autopilot." When we are not actively thinking, our brain is typically in a Default Mode Network state. For example, have you ever driven to a grocery store and forgotten where you parked your car when you leave? During those moments of placing your car in an appropriate spot, your mind is in a Default Mode Network. It automatically works to put a car in an acceptable place in the parking lot. Your brain just does the task.

A fundamental principle of our Default Mode Network is that our brain prefers being in this state and doesn't like to have exert any further energy. When we are actively pursuing new thoughts, new ideas, or new behaviors, our brain needs to exert energy. In this state, our brain is pumping cerebral barbells, shredding our limited beliefs, and entering into circuit training for the intellect. Our brain doesn't like it. It will resist these steps by making us more frustrated, more anxious, more mentally fatigued, more drained, or a list of other unpleasant experiences.

An important part of our Default Mode Network includes our Ventral Tegmental Area. This region of our brain secretes a specific neurohormone called dopamine. In life, we love and live for dopamine. It is our "reward" hormone. It is released when individuals use cocaine. It is released when one discovers something new. It is a hormone released when we go on vacations and experience something. It is also released when we have a pleasant surprise.

When we are functioning in our Default Mode Network, our brain is limited in the number of unique ways it knows how to secrete dopamine. Past experiences of pleasure remind us of ways to help the Ventral Tegmental Area to secrete dopamine. This natural phenomenon can wreak havoc on those who suffer from addictive disorders. The substance abuser's brain has been exposed to an experience (e.g., cocaine) that created pleasure. The substance abuser's brain in default mode, will take the path of least resistance to get more dopamine released...go find me more cocaine!

The problem gets even more complicated for the substance abuser. There is a neuroanatomic part of our brain that helps calm down our Ventral Tegmental Area. It is known as the inferior frontal lobe. This region of our brain does a great job helping to calm down an overly excited Ventral Tegmental Area. For those who have learned not to impulsively react to "drug cues," they have probably learned to harness the power of their inferior frontal lobes.

Unfortunately, for many of those involved with addictive disorders, their inferior frontal lobes might not be working so well. Drugs and alcohol are poisonous toxins to the brain. Chronic use of addictive agents may result in the inferior frontal lobes being traumatized such that they don't work so well.

In order to correct this problem, our brain needs time to rehabilitate. Hence, our inferior frontal lobes need to be placed in a nourishing, enriched environment so that they can be restored to their maximum capacity. If a gardener hopes to create home-grown vegetables, he or she will need healthy compost added to planter's soil, high-quality nitrogenous fertilizer and a correct balance of pure water. In a similar manner, your frontal lobes are going to need a nutrient-enriched habitat so that they have the most optimal capacity to function.[1]

Scheduling and Our Brain's Physiology

So what does our Ventral Tegmental Area and our Inferior Frontal Lobe have to do with scheduling? Scheduling is a way to begin to create a more nourished environment for our Inferior Frontal Lobe to flourish and grow. In order for our frontal lobe to become stronger, we need to start giving it biologically, psychologically, socially, and spiritually what it needs. Scheduling strengthens and fortifies our frontal lobe's ability to work at its best.

At its core, scheduling helps to expand our Default Mode Network's ability to find healthier ways to secrete dopamine. Many of our negative feelings about scheduling--it's childish, cumbersome, boring, and meaningless--are really a false message from our current Default Mode Network telling us not to change. Your brain has already figured out ways to secrete dopamine. Your Default Mode Network does not need more experiences to secrete dopamine; scheduling takes too much time and is energy-consuming for your brain.

What are the Benefits of Scheduling?

So what happens when we go against the grain of our well-established Default Mode Network and start to schedule? First, we start to develop a sense of accomplishment. Accomplishment is powerful. Accomplishment is the embodiment of what one experiences when an undesirable or unfathomable task is completed. After finishing a task or project, your Ventral Tegmental Area starts secreting dopamine. This dopamine gives you the intoxicating rush of a job well done. Rather than using illicit substances, your schedule becomes the "novel drug" giving you pleasure.

For example, I have worked with individuals suggesting that they spend at least one hour of day working out in order that they achieve a healthier weight. Loss of excess fat becomes a new feedback loop. As these individuals start to lose weight (and I have seen this happen fairly quickly with some individuals) they experienced a sense of accomplishment. Accomplishment leads to dopamine secretion. Dopamine leads to pleasure, pride, a new confidence, and most importantly, a desire to continue doing these constructive behaviors.

I treated another patient who was already in great shape and decided on adding something different on his schedule. He decided to renovate a room in a backyard trailer such that he could live in it. By adding one time slot per day for this project, my patient quickly began seeing a musty, dirty, and dilapidated dwelling place become a warm, comfortable, and aesthetic place to reside. What happened? His brain started secreting more dopamine! He felt proud, more confident, and refreshed.

More dopamine means we sense more accomplishment. More accomplishment reinforces further scheduling. More scheduling helps rehabilitate our frontal cortex and gives new experiences for our Ventral Tegmental Area to secrete dopamine. This is the type of cycle that scheduling can start to reinforce.

Next, creating a schedule gives us a sense of purpose. Purpose is meaning. It is life. It is invigoration. It is what keeps us up at night. It is what wakes us early in the morning. Purpose is that passionate idea that makes you and the world a better place.

Purpose does not find you. You have to actively look for it. How do we go about doing that? Pursue purpose by seeking out areas of active enjoyment. Where do you start? Put potential pleasurable activities on your schedule. Then, toy with them. Play with them. Experiment with them. Start to commit some time in your daily life to discover new opportunities for the sole purpose of finding enjoyment. This does not have to be overly complicated. It does not have to be overly expensive. You can do something as simple as finding a free cooking seminar, visit a local aquarium, watch a sporting event at a local park, or attend a local book club.

All of these experiences open the door for discovery and adventure. Once we discover something we genuinely enjoy, we begin to get close to what some might call transcendence. Transcendence brings us a unique pleasure. Transcendence helps secrete (guess what?)...dopamine! Subsequently, transcendence becomes another new reinforcing agent that promotes the need to have a great schedule.

As scheduling serves as a "seek and learn" mission to find passion, it also gives our brains something to look forward to experiencing. With a daily small list of "to dos" in front of us, our brain is less likely to return to its default mode setting. When we have free time alone, our mind tends to wander to its routine settings. Our brain likes those settings. It is used to them. It's easier. It doesn't have to exert a lot of energy.

When we finish a task on our schedule and see another upcoming "adventure," we play a great trick on our default mode network. Our brain doesn't have time to go back to its "old habits." Instead, it has something else new and exciting to experience. Our brain does not have time to get lazy. It has to prepare for something new and invigorating. Our brain does not have time to revert to negative thought patterns. It is too busy trying to understand how to think in novel and challenging situations.

A recent study on happiness published in the "Harvard Business Review" cogently backs up this concept. In this study, the researchers surprisingly found that the one activity that created the most unhappiness was mind wandering. When did peoples' minds wander the most? When they were alone, by themselves, doing nothing! Scheduling helps prevent mind wandering. It constructively deceives our brains into staying away from the default mode settings.

Not only does scheduling guide us down nature's path of contentment, it removes "the rocks of despair" and the "deep roots of negativity" so our brains can personally grow. We'll be discussing this very important aspect in an upcoming chapter. For now, it is important to know that personal growth means that one expands life experiences to promote personal discovery. Discovery leads to "OMG" and "ah-ah!" moments. These brief flashes are fun. They are intoxicating. They are liberating. And guess what else? We are secreting more...dopamine!

Where Do You Start?

One of the initial barriers that we often see in watching people develop schedules is that they find the task too laborious and time-consuming. "How can I fill 12 one-hour slots on my schedule every day?" "That's a lot of activities." "I don't even know that many things to do." "I have not even started and I already feel overwhelmed." "Even if I fill all my 'schedule squares,' I can't possibly follow this kind of schedule. So, why even start?"

These are all reasonable questions. They poke sound holes on creating any kind of schedule. Indirectly, the questions skeptically doubt our brain's ability to be creative, persistent, and flexible.

Rather than giving into our Default Mode Network's attempt to not even start, let's trick it! Let's play some deceptive (but very constructive) mind games of our own.

If someone were to ask you to fill out an hourly schedule, 12 hours per day, for one week, that comes to a grand total of 84 activities that you are going to need to put on your calendar! Eighty-four activities? That's a lot of activities! It is no wonder that are brains are so antagonistic to even want to start.

Instead of trying to fill up one-hour slots, I suggest doing something a bit differently. Beginning this adventure, let's break our day into three four-hour segments: morning, afternoon, and evening. In each of those sectors, just put one activity to do. Now we don't have 84 overwhelming assignments per week. We only have 21! Our brains can handle that.

To be even slyer with our Default Mode, let's say that each activity does not have to last the entire four hours ("Four hours; that's a long time! Why even start?"). It can be for as short as 30 minutes; just make sure it is written clearly, legibly, and distinctly on your schedule. Then, get even craftier. The activity does not necessarily all involve hard work (but I would suggest some). Just make sure that the activities are creative, productive, balanced, and engaging.

By setting up this type of schedule, you are shredding apart all of the self-defeating, lame excuses your Default Mode Network can and will give you to prevent you from even starting. For those of you used to arguing, fussing, complaining, and fighting, this is the type of real battle you are going to want to be actively engaged: the one inside of your head. So, let's get moving forward.

Back to Will

Remember how we started this chapter talking about Will? Will was resistant and definitely in a Default Mode Network state when we began to discuss scheduling. Here's what we did to help counteract some of his initial resistances.

First, Will decided to spend at least one hour (not four hours) in the morning working out. He would either go to the gym to lift weights, perform cardiovascular exercises, or do core training. Four weeks later, I saw Will. He had lost 20 pounds in one month. When he came to the office, it was hard to recognize this was the same "homeless Will" I saw 30 days earlier.

Subsequently, Will began to recognize the power of experiencing accomplishment. Although he found it hard to describe his internal state, Will just knew that he was becoming more confident and more self-assured. The quick feedback he got from losing weight helped him begin to believe that he could actually be healthier.

As Will continued to do his morning exercises, he decided to work on a trailer outside of his mother's home during the afternoon. Will decided that he would like to live in the trailer. However, the trailer was in shambles. It was dirty, leaking water, and needed significant painting. Will spent an afternoon putting a sealant on the roof. As mundane as this chore had been, Will began to see the short-term results of the internal trailer becoming dry and water free. As a result, Will was getting excited about the possibility of having his own personal "pad."

These pleasurable experiences motivated Will to start scraping paint off of the walls. In addition, he started going to different home renovation stores in the afternoons to look at potential wood floors that he would like to place in his new dwelling. Will was getting more inspired. Will was starting to believe in himself. Additionally, Will was developing his frontal cortex and finding constructive ways for his brain to secrete dopamine! This process was happening all due to the power of accomplishment.

These productive changes began to have a "snowball" like effect. Over the next two months, Will lost another 20 pounds! Now, Will was back to his high school weight. He was pleasantly surprised how different he was looking. This aesthetic presentation gave him confidence and more composure.

In addition, Will began to find a greater purpose beyond working out at the gym. Because of his transformative growth, Will wanted to have other people have similar transcending experiences. Eventually he began to explore the idea of getting a degree in performance training. In addition, Will wanted to go to college and get a degree in kinesthesiology (the study of musculature).

Finally, Will has also started communication about becoming a Navy Seal. This potential growth and development step surprised even me. Here was somebody who six months earlier was a substance abuser, living on the street, that could not afford rent, who was now looking to serve his country all because he decided to take better care of his brain?

How important is scheduling? Will was beginning to see the power of what can happen when we start to develop our own personalized schedules.

In closing this chapter, I hope that you will go against the grain of your Default Mode Network and try to develop your own personalized schedule. Start slow and simple. But most important, just start! I would also suggest picking activities where you see quick constructive results. By being able to observe constructive changes, your Ventral Tegmental area will start to naturally secrete dopamine resulting in you feeling better about yourself.

Summary

1. Creating a schedule can appear burdensome, excessive, and childlike for an adult to do.

2. Our brain's Default Mode Network naturally desires the path of least resistance. It does not like to exert any more energy than is necessary.

3. A schedule causes our brain to exert more energy. As a result, our Default Mode Network does not like it.

4. Yet, a schedule gives our brain the guidance and structure it needs to produce long-lasting positive change.

5. Creating a schedule helps build moments of accomplishment, a powerful experience that leads to long-lasting change.

6. Creating a schedule helps build a sense of purpose.

7. Creating a schedule keeps our brain busy by giving it growth-promoting activities to look forward to experiencing.

Questions

1. What are some of the initial reactions that come into your mind when you think of creating a schedule?
2. If you were to create a schedule, what are some of the possible advantages?
3. If you were to create a schedule, do you think that you could really stay committed to following through? What are some of the possible barriers?
4. How many days do you think you could realistically pull off creating a schedule and doing the activities you wrote down? What if you miss an activity? What would you typically say to yourself? What could you do to get back on track?
5. What are some activities that you could put on your schedule? Write down at least 20 activities (yep, 20 activities!).
6. Who could you go to for guidance if you can't think of activities to put on your schedule?
7. Who could be a key person to help you stay accountable to your schedule? How open would you be to asking for that support? Be honest.
8. Where might you find a good calendar that meets your preferential taste (paper, electronic, phone app)? If you can't afford a calendar, how might you obtain one?
9. How much do you value following through on the activities you wrote down on the calendar? (This is tough, but be honest with yourself.) How do you assess activities that you complete if you want to do them again?
10. How long do you perform an activity before you decide that it is not to your taste? How will you go about replacing it with another activity?
11. What feelings come up with activities you initially see as meaningless? How do you follow through and stay committed to finishing it? (Hey, you committed in writing to do the activity.)
12. What does accomplishment feel like? How could you discover its power by following through on your schedule?
13. When you have an upcoming activity that you are looking forward to, how do you feel? What thoughts come up in your mind?
14. If you don't have any upcoming activities planned, how do you feel? What kind of thoughts arise in your mind?

NOTES

CHAPTER 2

Self-Esteem

For those of you that have a smartphone, there have been a number of new games that can be downloaded and played (at least initially) free of charge. One app that is getting lots of attention is Candy Crush. In this game, the player has to knock out all of the jellies, candies, and fruits to get to the next level.

Although the rules are simple to quickly grasp, the complexity of the game is very engaging. Like many computer-modulated games, the goal is to win the current level in order to get to the next stage. The game does not have 10 levels. It does not have 50 levels. It doesn't even have 100 levels. There are currently 575 levels that need to be won!

When one first starts playing the initial lower levels of this game, the skill set needed to win is quite low. After a couple of minutes of playing, the participant "zaps" all the candies and "boom"...on to the next level. After winning the first 10 levels, you begin to feel like a real champion, leading to increased engagement. That novel connection results in players investing more time trying to get to even higher levels.

One interesting aspect of Candy Crush is that the game gives you "five free lives" per day. Typically, most players take these five daily lives for granted. You download a free app. You are playing, supposedly, a free game. You should get lots (heaps, tons, oodles) of free lives! Why? Because the game is free. It said so when you downloaded it. Right?

Well, not necessarily. This is where the game gets rather interesting. As lives are lost, the attitudes of players can change. Some contestants become more frustrated, not liking to lose…at all; some start to question their overall competence wondering what is wrong with them when trying to get to the next level; some get dismayed wondering if they will be able to keep up with their friend's level of play; and some see it just as a game: they are having fun; if all lives are lost, they can come back tomorrow for more enjoyment.

Financially, the game developers hope that the players will take their loss of lives more personally. For the frustrated, down-trodden, overly competitive, the designers have set up a system to deal with that internal turmoil. Just pay an extra 99 cents via your credit card and you can have additional lives. For those who are personally invested (or maybe just highly addicted), market data has shown that they will pay the price to keep on going. How much are these overly charged players willing to pay? A lot! Recently, an article came out in the local news about players paying over $1,000 per month for these additional lives.1 Those small 99 cent incremental payments can add up rather quickly.

Our self-esteem is in many ways like the experience of losing those "five daily free lives." A lost Candy Crush life could be a relationship gone sour; it could represent not being able to pay all your bills; it could reflect a job interview that did not result in being hired. Life can and will throw curve balls at you. It is at these moments that you will find out who you really are.

This is where self-esteem is so pivotal. During the good times, it is easy to take our self-esteem for granted. It is in those tough times, though, when our "five Candy Crush lives" run out; it is then when we discover the true inner core of our being. And in these moments, you can't pay "99 cents" (or thousands of dollars) to boost your ego. You either have high esteem, with a strong fighting spirit to keep moving forward, or, you don't.

If you don't have the added surplus of high self-esteem during the tough times, more negative results can and will happen. Without a high level of self-respect, you are going to be more willing to give up. If you aren't working on being genuinely proud, you are more at risk to suddenly throw a major "tire blowout" temper tantrum. If you lack resilience and abruptly get asked to leave your group home, you might find yourself going back to your "woe is me" addictive habits as a means to escape.

So what is the end result in acting out in these ways? You will be a lot more likely to end up going back to a place you really want to avoid…jail! Self-esteem may seem soft. It may appear trite. Its essence may seem weak, meaningless…a lot of "psycho-babble."

Yet, the very foundation of self-esteem is going to make you stronger. It will push you beyond the hurdles that will lay before you. It will give you the courage to pursue goals that don't seem possible. It will demand that you become more accountable and make something out of yourself. Self-esteem is not fluffy. It is not feeble. It is not frail.

Self-esteem is strong. It is tough. It is the steel of your soul.

How Does Low Self-Esteem Present Itself?

The issue of possessing high or low self-esteem can be difficult. How do you know if you have high or low self-esteem? What qualities, beliefs, and mannerisms demonstrate an affirmative belief in oneself?

For those getting released from jail/prison, the assumption from the external world is that you probably have low self-esteem. Whether that truly is the case will be up to the individual to decide.

Some factors that may distinguish those with low self-esteem have been mentioned above. When in the face of adversity, how does one handle the inherent stress involved? Should you be one who becomes readily angry, gives up in defeat, or, even worse, starts feeling sorry for yourself, there are most likely some opportunities for improvement.

If you aren't open to criticism or suggestions from others, be very watchful of yourself. Should you dismiss other's suggestions, turn off your listening skills, or be silently telling yourself, "This person is an idiot; I know more than they do," you might not be so comfortable in your own skin.

In addition to projecting fault on others, some insecure individuals will often run away from opportunities for improvement. They will change topics, become overly "cocky" to avoid unpleasant feelings, or exaggerate accomplishments hoping others will not notice their weaknesses.

Most concerning is the person who will solely blame others for their woes. They are not the problem. It is the system, the spouse, the mother, the father, or any other entity...besides them. "Breaks in life have just not come my way." "If only people had taken the time to really get to know me." "It's not me. It is unfortunate circumstances have not given me more hopeful opportunities."

Should you be of this belief system, kindly take the time to review the five skill sets below needed to have high self-esteem. If you can honestly say that you are practicing these disciplines daily, then you may be humbly giving an honest appraisal of yourself. If not, then it is time to learn new ways to increase your level of self-respect.

So What Exactly is Good Self-Esteem?

Best-selling author, Nathaniel Brandon, has written a number of books on self-esteem. From his observations, he sees two important qualities in those with high self-regard.

First, individuals with high self-esteem have the "confidence to think and cope with the challenges of life."[2] As mentioned above, when road blocks occur, then those of high self-respect take safe "off-street detours" remaining flexible and confident that they can meet their goals. There is not any whining. There is not any complaining. There is not any negativity. Instead, there is a flexible willingness to change. In addition, there is a renewed optimism that this current change of plan will lead to a better result.

Second, those with high self-esteem possess an unabashed "confidence in one's own inherent right to be happy. They have a right to feel worthy and, as a result, are entitled to assert one's needs and wants as well as enjoy the fruits of hard efforts."[3] There is a great deal being said in this small sentence so we will break it down.

Individuals with high esteem have a confidence in their right to be happy and feel worthy. Confidence is a pure genuine tangibly felt experience. It is not pre-fabricated. It is not made up. It is not a mass of "verbal hype." Confidence is real; either you have it or you don't.

Next, individuals with high self-esteem readily distinguish and respect the differences between internal happiness and the external accumulation of wealth. Money, luxury, and elegant goods are nice to have. However, they don't necessarily create genuine self-respect. Those with high self-regard don't necessarily avoid obtaining financial wealth. They, instead, recognize that there are different fundamental practices that can and must be done to improve one's self-esteem.

That being said, your inherent right to possess happiness and high self-worth demands that you work hard practicing those skill sets in order to attain it. There is no "snap of your fingers" self-entitled right to happiness. This will take some energy. It will take some time. It will take some patience. The harder you work at the sound practices of being important, the more likely you will be to start finding internal self-worth.

As we continue to dig deeper into Brandon's conceptualization of healthy self-esteem, another important characteristic is noted. Those with healthy self-worth recognize that they are entitled to assert their needs and wants. "Entitled" is an interesting word here and can be taken out context. Entitled gives one the assurance that they have the privilege to communicate their genuine desires. This guarantee also implies that the communicator has a sincere respect and appreciation for those needs being communicated. That being said, one's entitled right to assert does not mean that those desires will be immediately met. Instead, the privilege fundamentally allows the individual to sincerely, wholeheartedly, and authentically express his or her true desires.

"Entitled" has become a phrase programmed into the American culture to mean that if you are entitled to something, you should get it...automatically. A college graduate wrote a poem after graduating from college. It focused on how the media, culture, and friends had preprogrammed him into a false reality. All the student needed to do was go to college, work hard, and he  would fulfill his multimillionaire Hollywood actor dream. After finishing his undergraduate work, reality led to painful disgruntlement. He realized that being entitled to go after your dreams doesn't mean that you are going to automatically get your most passionate desires. Rather than getting bitter about "being screwed", he became more engaged. Happiness, he realized, was an internal quest of harnessing discipline, hard work, and passion. His entitlement was the pursuit of that internal state; not some self-righteous, self-deserving lifestyle.

Finally, high self-esteem meant that you have the right to enjoy the hard work of your efforts. Of note, this statement does not say you have the right to enjoy the results of your efforts. The end byproduct may or may not be what you expected. The outcome may not necessarily bring what you are hoping. The final reward may not be as much as you wanted.

Moreover, results are not controllable. Hence, why would anyone want to commit to defining your self-regard by how much you get? You don't have any control over that.

The only control you really do have is over what you can give. Giving comes from putting forth hard work. Hard work will lead to an internal sense of fulfillment. That fulfillment will give you a higher regard and respect for yourself. You will go through mud. You will go through dirt. You will push yourself beyond what you ever expected. It is at those moments that you will become something greater, whether you receive an instantaneous reward or not.

Passionately work hard. Immerse your heart in giving your very best. It is at these times that you will truly discover what you can become. For those of you who have played sports, you might remember a coach who pushed you beyond what you thought was your breaking point. It is at these times that you can become internally aware of who you are becoming. That is true self-respect. Outcomes will not do it. Hard work will.

Why is it so Important to Develop High Esteem?

High self-esteem can certainly help you become a better friend to yourself. However, there are other reasons why self-esteem is extremely important to develop.

Your success will depend upon the personal relationships you develop and how you add value to them. Hence, your ability to develop personal camaraderie will tell you just how far you are going to go in life. So how does this skill relate to self-esteem?

Famed leadership author, John Maxwell, states that, "You teach people how to treat you." This is a very powerful statement. Your ability to receive self-respect is a byproduct of how well that you value yourself. If you don't like yourself, then people won't like you. If you think that you are inferior to other people, then they will see you as inferior. If you think that you are at a lower level, then others will perceive you at a lower level.

While some of you ponder this reality, you might argue that if you see yourself better than others, then others will see you at a higher status. Therefore, just act like you are greater than the person with whom you are speaking.

So let's take this one step further. When I was living in Los Angeles working out at my gym, a well-known actor of an Emmy Award-winning television show was doing some biceps exercises. I asked him a quick question to verify that it was him, to which he said "yes." I told the actor that I had grown up in Minnesota, and that he had been my favorite athlete on the local sports team. He started laughing, and said, "Boy, you are making me feel old." I laughed and stated that I was only five years younger than him. That broke the ice. I must've spoken to this person for about 45 minutes at the gym. We talked about a lot of his old teammates. We talked about some of the games that he was in. We also talked about fishing in Colorado. It was actually a really fun conversation.

As soon as we were done talking, another individual who I knew came up to this actor. This individual had a reputation for trying to connect with highly powerful people in Hollywood. In many ways, I was somewhat intimidated by him. I thought for sure that this actor would speak with him longer than myself. To my surprise, the actor blew him off. I was rather surprised and shocked. How could I have spoken to this person so long and had a great conversation while this other person got thrown to the side? (please note that I have some of my own self-esteem issues)

So I did some research. As I explored what occurred, I had never really known what this "cool" person at the gym had done for a living. It turns out that he didn't really have a job. He also had a lot of other personal issues, of which I will not elaborate, that he was not working to resolve. Instead, he took shortcuts thinking that if he made the right connections, then he could become as powerful. In essence, he had very low self-esteem.

You cannot fake high self-esteem. You either have it or you do not. Unfortunately, this person tried to demonstrate that he had just as much power as the actor. The result... It did not work. People can smell manipulators, liars, and phoniness long before it arrives. Additionally, the more successful people become, the more aware they become of others trying to use them.

The take-home message is this: you're going to have to sincerely work at your self-esteem. You are going to have to be honest with yourself. You are going to have to work on disciplines to internally feel better about yourself. Putting on a false pretense just plain won't cut it.

What are the Disciplines of Self-Esteem?

In order to work on a better sense of who you are, you are going to have to break it down in some simple, yet very demanding steps. Here are some pragmatic means to work on self-esteem.

1. Mastery

Mastery is the constant pursuit of becoming better in a skill, an attitude, or a belief system. The very essence of mastery is elusive. No matter how hard you try, you just don't quite reach it. Golf pros are notoriously talking about the need to improve their putting, their short game, their long irons, their sand game, and their pitching. Even though they may win great championships, they never quite get to mastery. You might get close, but you are never quite inside its doors.

So what makes mastery so important to our esteem if we never quite "get there"? Mastery teaches one how to focus. It forces our brain to remain diligent on only one topic and passionately pursue it just for the sake of getting better. Such work gets our brains out of our Default Mode Network and takes us on a journey to experience passion, commitment, and excellence.

There will be moments of frustration on this journey. There will be adversity, irritation, and strong desires to quit. Although being tempted to throw in the towel, anything worth doing well is worth doing poorly as well. The very fact that mastery will lead to frustration teaches our brains another important aspect of life. We can either quit working on getting better leading to "failure or disappointment," or instead, we can rise above our circumstances, producing determination, faith, and belief in ourselves.4

To get started, I would suggest picking a constructive activity that you might find enjoyable. This choice could involve playing tennis, being a comedian, reading novels, writing short stories, gardening, carpentry, photography, etc. If you aren't sure what you might enjoy, then ask someone for help. Ask your parole officer, your counselor, a family member, or a friend. Even if you aren't 100 percent sure, just pick something. You can always change.

Next, decide each day to learn something extra about that activity and practice it. Extra is the key word here. Push yourself to learn and do more. You may feel awkward, uncomfortable, and unrewarded. But you are also going to feel engaged, connected, focused, and energized. Your brain won't be passive. It is too busy trying to integrate all the new material that you have put in front of it. It will become more vibrant and alive, feeling refreshed as you get better giving that extra.

2. Consciousness

Consciousness is the purposeful attempt to get a better understanding of our feelings, behaviors, and thoughts as well as expanding them. The key here is to expand. It is not enough to become aware of our (for most of us) negative thoughts, unpleasant feelings, and regretful behaviors. We need to move beyond them. We need to broaden what we are cultivating in our internal garden. We need to pick the weeds, prune the thickets, and get rid of the sage brush such that we can plant some Rocky Mountain aspens, nurture some Georgia longleaf pines, grow colorful cadenza roses, and seed tropical birds of paradise.

In order to have a better horticultural experience, we have to quit asking momentum-stopping questions. Such inquiries include "Why do I always think so negatively?", "Why are other people always seeming to do better them me?", or "What activities did I do yesterday?" These questions will paralyze us. They will inhibit our minds from being more vibrant and alive. They keep us living in the lives of our past.

Instead, it is important that you ask for assertive directive questions using the words "should" or "could."5 "What could I focus on right now that could help me grow and accrue?" Faith? Love? Trust? Confidence? "What types of emotions do others feel that I wish I experienced more?" Joy? Laughter? Lightheartedness? What constructive behaviors do I really envy in others that I could attain? Persistence? Staying physically fit? A sense of humor?

Consciousness is not a passive psychoanalytic reflection of where you have been. It is an active pursuit that propels your mind to places it has never been. The experience generates energy to lift one into new creative horizons. Consciousness is creative. Consciousness is life-giving. Consciousness is power.

To start working on this discipline, I would suggest getting an 8.5 inch by 11 inch notebook and start journaling your thoughts using "should" and "could" questions. You will know that you are making progress when you start pursuing constructive thoughts, emotions, behaviors, and beliefs that you have not experienced in the past.

3. Purposefulness

Purposefulness is the daily pursuit of making life meaningful. For many individuals, this is not their typical existence. Instead, they are survivalists. "How can I just get through the monotony of this day?" "How many more mundane working days before the weekend arrives?" "How many more hours before I get a coffee break from this ho-hum job?" For these non-existent souls, "life is motion without meaning, activity without direction, and events without a reason. Without a purpose, life is trivial, petty and pointless."6 For those of you who just have been released from jail or prison, these words may cling to how life has been living behind bars. Unfortunately, the survivalist mentality continues for those even after they have left their 8 feet by 8 feet cells. Life is boring. Life is dull. Life is listless.

As sad as it is to see so many living this non-heroic lifestyle, there is hope. There is optimism. There is a way out. Why? Because having a purpose does not cost a lot of money to obtain. Finding a purpose can actually be discovered. Pursuing a purpose doesn't have to drain one of their emotional and cognitive energy.

So how does one find "their purpose"? It begins by asking one simple question: "What can I (and only I) do to make life a better place than when I came into it?" This question is powerful. By exploring and eventually finding an answer, you will learn about personal power, internal motivation, never-ending passion, and unstoppable adversity.

Your purpose is unique. Your purpose is special. Your purpose only pertains to YOU. Furthermore, your mind and soul will be engaged. Life won't be boring. Life won't be dull. Life won't be listless. It will be an adventure with continual discoveries.

As you start or continue your current journaling habit, the purpose question would be a great place to jot down your thoughts, find your purpose, and harmonize your behaviors toward that great endeavor.

4. Letting Go

When I was in tenth grade, my parents had "forced" me to go to a summer camp that I was not excited to attend. About one month before the departure date, the counselors presented a film about the camp. In it, the hired commentator audaciously said, "This will be the greatest experience you have ever had in your life." At the end of this 30-minute propagandized promotion, my adolescent cynical side was about to burst, "Come on, I may only be a sophomore in high school, but I am not stupid enough to believe this 'spin,' I thought."

Grudgingly, I went to the weeklong camp. It was a church camp (I was not the most spiritual person at that time), which added even more skepticism to my preconceived ideas of what to expect. On the night before leaving, I consciously used my young, masculine 15-year-old "quiet time" to demonstratively declare what would be important to me on this trip. Here were my intellectually inspiring priorities: What competitive activities would we be doing (no silly games-no Twister, no darts, etc.)? What delectable foods would they be serving (no tuna casserole, spaghetti hot dish, etc.)? And, most important, how attractive and approachable would the girls be?

That was it. I wanted fun. I craved action. I demanded adventure. I was on a quest for dates. My young, rebellious mind was made up what I would focus on these three areas. I would have a great attitude no matter what was thrown at me.

When we finally got to camp, I was quite surprised. On the first night, we were served fresh roasted turkey (not the tasteless pressed type) with mashed potatoes. On my first spoonful of mashed potatoes, I thought for sure they would be those cheesy, cheap, powdered potatoes. Nope, they were the real thing. "Hey, this is actually a lot better than the school cafeteria food."

The next morning at breakfast, I was just waiting to get some disappointment thrown at me. I suspiciously knew...I just knew it would be a boring breakfast...something like plain instant oatmeal. Well, I was wrong again. No oatmeal...what is this? "What, they are feeding us strawberry crepes? Come on, there has to be a glitch here somewhere. We are probably only going to get to eat three of them. What? We can eat as much as we want? Yeah! This is great!"

As for activities, I was just holding my breath. I grew up playing varsity sports. The last thing that I wanted was to be rope-tied leg-to-leg with someone competing in a weird three-legged race. I was already imagining winning the stupid race hearing the false cheering, "Congrats, you won. Way to go! You are so good." Internally, I would be saying to myself, "Whoopee. Who the heck cares? This is so stupid!"

Well, we never had the three-legged race. In fact, we did not have Twister either. Instead, we had these intense volleyball tournaments with dudes from other states that were 6 feet 5 inches tall just slamming spikes across the nets. While we played, all the campers from respective high schools started cheering for their teams. This was great. This was varsity sports at another level. I loved competition, and the last thing I wanted to do was to lose against some weak out-of-state high school team.

Then, we had to go hiking. My initial sarcastic thoughts were, "Oh, this will be cute; we will spend an hour meandering up some bluff and traverse down faking that this was really hard. Whew! I am so tired. I think I need to take a nap."

Well, guess what? I was wrong again. Instead of climbing up a small hill a few hundred yards high, I was taken on an eight hour excursion climbing to the top of a 14,204 feet Rocky Mountain peak! The hike was painful. One kid almost died accidentally sliding 1,500 feet down a patch of snow. I had three asthma attacks getting to the top. This was physically hard. It was excruciating. It hurt. And I loved every minute of it. When we finally reached the peak, I can't even describe the feeling. The views were breathtaking. I felt like I had really accomplished something.

And finally, my juvenile concerns about what potential phone numbers I could bring home were not disappointed. I grew up in the North and the camp had "drafted" all these teen beauties from the South. The experience helped me truly appreciate the meaning of "Southern Belles." To this day, I still can remember flirting away with one girl who looked like Miss Teen USA Texas and getting her digits. "Yeah, baby. Wow, this place is insane!"

With all my expectations surprisingly met, the camp also took me on yet another very special, and more important journey. This place allowed me to safely explore my spirituality, my personal insecurities, and how I could become a better person. This adventure was all done in a very emotionally respectful environment without criticism, harshness, or ridicule.

As the week came to end, I did not want to leave. This place was special. It was inspiring. It was magic. And 40 years later as I write out this memoir, the film I saw before going to camp was right. The week at camp was the greatest experience in my first 16 years of life.

So what made it so special? Why was it unique? When I returned home and reflected, it wasn't because I was fed chargrilled steaks, fresh vegetables, and homemade pies. It wasn't because we were competing in sports at the same level as our high school conferences. And it wasn't because I would have some great stories about all the beautiful women I met.

The camp was special because they allowed me to let go. I could naturally and genuinely just be myself. I was accepted. I was allowed to make mistakes. I was allowed to be...free.

In order to let go, you are going to need to release of all of the negative self-talk. You need to recognize it, own it, and then let it go. Replace negativity with encouragement, limiting beliefs with empowering statements, and personal insecurities with validating truisms.

In addition to putting the negative self-trash-talking in the incinerator, you are going to need to learn to forgive yourself. Don't expect others to give you that opportunistic break. They won't. Besides, it would not matter anyway...if you don't do it for yourself first.

Next, you will have to learn how to naturally be yourself. No drugs allowed! Naturally is the key word here. Learn to laugh. Learn to have fun. Learn to just be you.

Finally (we will talk further about this later), find friends, family, and support people who unconditionally accept you for who you are. They are the cast of characters who will be your biggest cheerleaders during the tough times. Being in that environment will raise your esteem, your potential, and satisfaction in life.

Summary

1. Our self-esteem is an internal representation that reflects how we see, think, and feel about ourselves.
2. That internal viewpoint is best reflected when we are under some type of stress or adversity.
3. Our self-esteem will direct how we guide ourselves during that tenacious time.
   a. If we have a belief that we aren't worthwhile, overly confident, or capable, then we will naturally quit and succumb to the obstacle.
   b. If we have a belief that we are significant, strong, and have something special to offer life, then we will naturally fight during those tougher times.
4. Our self-esteem is not something that is stagnant. It either grows or withers depending how we nurture it.
5. It is important that we develop our self-esteem in order that we can successfully overcome the hurdles of life.
6. In order to improve our self-worth, it is important that we work on the following disciplines:
   a. Mastery
   b. Consciousness
   c. Purposefulness
   d. Letting Go

Questions

1. When you think of all the individuals who talked about self-esteem in your life, what types of concepts and feeling arise in your mind?
2. How might having improved self-esteem help you in your life?
3. Who are some people who you have met that have demonstrated good self-esteem? If you can't think of any, what about people on the news, television, or movies?

4. Kevin Costner playing Crash Davis in "Bull Durham," a great movie of some-one working daily to improve his self-esteem in the many quagmires of life. If possible, watch the movie. Then, ask yourself what Crash Davis did in the movie to improve his self-respect. What were the results? How could you incorporate some of his disciplines in your own life?

5. What is an area in your past that you have tried to master? How well did you do? What could you have done differently? What is an area that you could work on now to intentionally move towards mastery?

6. If you cannot think of an area, what, instead, happened? How has that shaped you? What beliefs developed later on? How could you change those beliefs? How can you find an area now to master?

7. If you already know, what is the purpose of your life? If you are not sure, how could you start to discover it? (This is hard work but there is lots of good material out to assist.)

8. If it is indeed true that our self-esteem can wax and wane, what were some times in your life when your self-esteem was low? When were there some peaks? What was going on during those peaks? How could you work towards creating more peaks?

9. Think of a time that was very stressful in your life. What was going on? How were you feeling? How did you behave? How would you have rated your self-esteem? What might have you done differently back then? How could you incorporate some of those skill sets now in your life?

10. Have there been any times in your life when you actually felt emotionally safe? If so, what were they like? Who were the people? What were those indi-viduals doing? How can you find ways to incorporate that in your life now?

11. If there have not been many emotionally safe experiences, how might we discover them? Where can we go to find them? What types of people should we be looking for to let go and just be yourself?

12. What emotions and beliefs do you experience the majority of the time?

13. How could you expand your emotions and beliefs to be more inclined to-ward constructive values...confidence, excellence, self-control, integrity, etc.?

14. What are some of your current hurdles? If you had lower self-esteem than the current moment, how would you act? If you had much higher self-esteem how would you act?

15. Who is someone famous you have heard of that has high self-esteem? Pretend that they are currently dealing with your dilemmas (lack of job, minimal support, cramped living quarters, etc.). If they were walking in your boots now, what would they be doing differently? Pick one of your answers and playfully experiment to see what happens.

NOTES

CHAPTER 3

Sobriety

On February 2, 2014, Philip Seymour Hoffman was found dead in his apartment. Hoffman had taken an accidental overdose of a mixed drug intoxication. A syringe was found left in his arm containing heroin, benzodiazepines, cocaine, and amphetamines.1

Hoffman, a 46-year-old, Academy Award winning actor best known for his role in "Capote," had also been featured in many other feature length films including "Charlie Wilson's War," "Doubt," "The Master," and his latest, "Hunger Games."

Hoffman's sudden death represents the sharp sting of just how quickly the world of drugs, alcohol, and illicit substances can catch up to you. For the past 23 years, Hoffman had been living a lifestyle of sobriety, often showing up at New York City's self-help group meetings. His message was one of hope and optimism. Attended by countless substance abusers, Hoffman heroically communicated to those addicted that it was possible to stay away from perils and foibles of illicit substances.

Hoffman's unexpected relapse illustrates the potency of drug's seductive allure. His re-introduction to the drug world had not been very long. There had not been any chronic health problems. There had not been any legal arrests. There were no news flashes. There were no warning signs giving the public reason to silently assume, "This guy is heading for trouble." Hoffman's death was quick, sudden, and harsh.

Following the funeral, there was another story that began to emerge. Its theme represents the twists, turns, and unexpected negative surprises that often get associated with drugs.

Robert Vineberg, a 57-year-old musician friend of Hoffman, was thought to be responsible for supplying Hoffman with his recreational substances. Following

Hoffman's death, Vineberg was later arrested on a felony conviction of criminal possession of a controlled substance. The initiation of these charges were thought to be direct result of Vineberg allegedly supplying illicit substances to Hoffman.

Although there has not been much press about Vineberg's involvement and reaction, there would be reasonable speculation that he tried to cover all unwanted actions. Vineberg has been very successful. He is bright, talented, and well-known in the music industry. Given his high profile, it would be reasonable to assume that he would think of most, if not all, ill-desired consequences with drugs. Legally, make sure that you sell to only people you know. Financially, keep any earnings safely hidden from the government. Socially, use only with people who are wanting it for recreational purposes.

I am willing to bet that Vineberg felt like the rug was being pulled up under his feet. Hoffman's death was most likely one consequence that was not thought of in advance. He was merely doing Hoffman "a favor" making sure his buddy can have the lightness, spontaneity, and laughter of a "Hollywood Lifestyle."

The joviality came to a screeching halt. Vineberg was "devastated" by the sudden change of events. Who would have thought that this tragedy would have occurred from the often minimized seriousness of drugs?

Although Vineberg has not been convicted, the story illustrates the countless number of negative surprises that can happen around drugs. In this situation, I am willing to bet that Vineberg had not had any idea that something like this would happen. Sad to say, there are many other cataclysmic sagas that suddenly ignite when there is a close association with drugs and alcohol. Many substance abusers think that they have all angles covered. Unfortunately, drugs can be like black mold growing in a moist shower. No matter how hard you try to clean, remove, and disinfect this toxic substance, it has a way of slyly infesting other crevices and corners.

The purpose of including this chapter is help you not follow the unfortunate footsteps of Vineberg (and Hoffman). You don't want to become a voluntary victim of careless choices. Any association to drugs or alcohol can have serious repercussions.

The consequences often surprise the offender. They never saw it coming. And when the balloon bursts, the person involved often says to themselves "if only I would have thought this through better."

The rest of this chapter will help you never have to arrive at "if only." No passport, no free ticket, no voucher can take back from the harsh, cold, catastrophic unpleasantries associated with drugs.

Substance Abuse and the Criminal System

The association of drug use and criminal behavior is staggering. In 2010, the National Center on Addiction and Substance Abuse (CASA) conducted a study, The CASA Report, indicating that of the 2.2 million inmates in prisons and jails, 1.5 million prisoners had a DSM-IV Substance Abuse diagnosis. This means that 68 percent – significantly more than half - of our convicted criminals have a substance abuse problem.[2]

Increasing this epidemic dilemma, the study indicated another 458,000 inmates who did not meet strict DSM-IV criteria had either a history of substance abuse or were under the influence at the time of their crime. Adding it up, these numbers indicate that nearly 90 percent of all convicts have a substance use or abuse related problem!

Moreover, the CASA study indicated that only 11 percent of those incarcerated inmates who were diagnosed as suffering from an addictive disorder were receiving any treatment. So how does this lack of treatment effect the long-term outcome of this population? A study by Bahr et al. followed 53 parolees for three years to assess what kept them from going back to jail/prison. The study demonstrated that those who received substance abuse treatment while in jail and, in addtion, obtained subsequent emotional support from friends/family were more likely to still be out of prison in three years.[3]

If this data is indeed accurate, then why are we not treating more inmates in jail/prison such that they don't return? If finances to pay for services are a main issue, the CASA study would indicate a different story. The study denoted that such expenses would break even if just 10 percent of parolees abstained from illicit substances, held a job, and did not break the law. How long would the parolee have to follow these lifestyle strategies for the program to break even? Ten years? Five years? Two Years? No! If the parolee can keep out of trouble just one year, the services provided in jail/prison would pay for themselves.

Thereafter, that first year an inmate can remain sober, crime free, and employed, the CASA Study indicated that the nation would glean "an additional $90,953 per year.[4] If these numbers prove to be true, that would hypothetically mean that if only

200,000 inmates were to stay out of the system, an additional $18.2 billion would be saved. Hypothetically, if the nation were able to keep all two million inmates from going back into jail, the government would have an additional $182 billion savings in tax dollars per year. How would such funds help move us to a balanced national budget?

Psychiatric Disorders and the Criminal System

Because of the statistically high numbers, one can reasonably ask if these drug-dependent criminals have underlying brain pathology in addition to their behavioral problems. If so, should society be taking further efforts to incorporate brain rehabilitation accompanying criminal punishment?

Over the past two decades, there has been a substantial increased focus on this very topic. Non-invasive neuroimaging techniques such as SPECT scans, PET Scans, Quantitative EEGs, and fMRI's are beginning to unravel the complexities of brain functioning.

Notably, findings are indicating that many individuals incarcerated have a higher likelihood of brains that are either over- or under-functioning in specific neuroanatomical regions.7 For example, a study at the University of South Carolina assessing 636 prisoners indicated that 65 percent of males and 73 percent of females had suffered from a traumatic brain injury.5 These numbers indicate that the brain injury rate is seven times higher than that found in the general population.

Coupling the high substance abuse rate and the increased traumatic brain injuries, how and should society deal with these concerning numbers? Many who are incarcerated don't just demonstrate bad behaviors; they have sick brains. Our technologies are bringing this to light over the last decade. As a society, what are we to do? When an individual commits a criminal offense, should our institutions begin to assess if there is a substance abuse issue, a mental health illness, or a traumatic brain injury? If so, does society have an obligation to find ways to treat the pathological brain while the convict is simultaneously (and understandably) punished for their crime?

One reasonable argument against this approach is that the criminal will use his brain malfunctioning as a means to condone illegal behaviors. They won't take responsibility. They won't accept accountability. They will manipulate this concept to meet their own selfish needs.

During any type of therapeutic treatment plan, it will be important for the convict to understand that they need to take responsibility for their brain. Although they may not have asked for the brain they have (no one did), it is up to them to responsibly manage it. Respect it. Value it. Rehabilitate it. If one can't follow a detailed care plan to help their brain circuitry function better, then a more structured setting (i.e., prison) may be the most amenable approach.

At the Amen Clinics, where I work, we have seen some amazing changes when people are able to look at their brain and how it functions. Some of our most skeptical patients have developed what we call "brain envy." Brain envy is best described as a sudden change in disposition to have a healthier brain. After a patient sees a picture of their malfunctioning brain, many develop a strong desire to change. They see their unhealthy scans. They see healthy scans. OUCH! They don't like it. Subsequently, their denials, rationalizations, minimizations, and weak excuses start to diminish. They get a "live shot" of just how poorly things look upstairs. Suddenly, a strong urge to get their brain looking normal is set aflame.

If you are a prisoner, our highest hope is that you will take an approach to understand your brain functioning, take responsibility for it, and make it healthier. Change. Take constructive action. Work. Get an action plan in place to get your brain working better.

Neuroanatomy and Behavioral Change

How does one start to develop such an action plan? A great place to start is to get personally acquainted with your brain. Know what regions are working well. Become aware of what areas are not executing as well as they should. Develop appreciation for "pressure points" that might be overworking.

For example, a region of your brain known as the inferior frontal cortex plays a pivotal role in staying focused, making sound judgments, and completing tasks. The functionality of the inferior frontal cortex would be illustrated by an individual who comes up with an idea to build a fence around their yard. You start the project. You remain persistent and don't let the everyday forces of life stop you from finishing. You complete the project.

This part of your brain acts similarly to the paddles of a whitewater raft going down the Grand Canyon. Once rapids hit, you are bounced, tossed, and turned to the point of capsizing. The ride is invigorating…yet very dangerous. Head off in the wrong path and your boat becomes the passive recipient of the forces of nature. The end result…you lose, game over. Your raft has been shredded. Those paddles help you stay on course. They don't let the whims of roaring rapids overtake you. They guide. They direct. They keep you focused.

For the substance abuser with poor inferior frontal lobe functioning, the end results can be as devastating as the unchartered raft. Often after a period of staying sober, the substance abuser understandably begins to feel more confident about themselves. They have not used any illicit drugs for a significant time. They have a great support group. They feel in control. They have a sense of pride. They have more power.

Then, the "rapids" hit. A close friend calls and says that several buddies are going down to the local pub to play some pool. The invigorated and transformed abuser starts thinking, "Hey, this will be fun. I know that I won't be drinking. I will just use my new skill sets to stay away from the liquor. Plus, it would be great to see everyone. And I will feel even better when I get home."

To some individuals working on sobriety, they may very well be able to abstain. They take their pool cue to shoot some "eight ball" (no, not cocaine!), joke around, drink some bottled water, and go home…end-of-story.

However, for the substance abuser with inferior frontal lobe problems, they will often take the meaning of white water rafting to a whole new turbulent level. Not only are they lacking good sturdy paddles, they likely don't even have a save life preserver should the raft capsize.

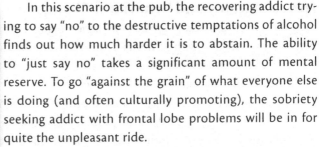

In this scenario at the pub, the recovering addict trying to say "no" to the destructive temptations of alcohol finds out how much harder it is to abstain. The ability to "just say no" takes a significant amount of mental reserve. To go "against the grain" of what everyone else is doing (and often culturally promoting), the sobriety seeking addict with frontal lobe problems will be in for quite the unpleasant ride.

The problem with these individuals with poor frontal lobe functioning is that they don't have the reserve capacity to face the challenge head on and say, "No. I am not going down that path." Instead, what happens to these well-meaning sobriety seekers? "Well, I will just have one drink so I can fit in. One drink won't hurt." Do they have just one drink? No! They have several shots and end up getting severely intoxicated.

The following morning, the hung over abuser starts to think, "What the heck happened? Am I that weak? Am I that soft? Do I need to be treated like I am a child and not be allowed to go to adult places?" Guilt, dismay, and regret start to slowly creep into all the cracks and crevices of trying to live a sober lifestyle.

As unpleasant as these subsequent feelings appear, the most painful emotion is shame. Shame attacks our core. It penetrates deeply into our inner soul. It rips our sense of identity to pieces.

Sadly, shame's poignant finger pointing labeling one's soul, inner core, or identity wasn't the real problem. It was their low functioning inferior frontal lobes! They aren't working well. They were running low on fuel. They needed more time to develop. Once the substance abuser grasps the concept that they are not some immoral, sickly self-indulging, weak soul, they can make some profound steps forward. Rather than fermenting in harsh self-reproach or feeling sorry for oneself, the substance abuser can take full accountability to improve their low functioning inferior frontal lobes. They need to respect their inferior frontal lobes. They need to nurture them. They need to rehabilitate them to health.

Dr. Daniel Amen's "10 Principles of Brain Health"

1. **Your Brain Is Involved In Everything You Do.**
2. **When Your Brain Works Right, You Work Right. When Your Brain Is Troubled, You Are More Likely To Have Trouble.**
3. **Your Brain Is The Most Amazing Organ In The Universe.**

4. Your Brain is Soft, About The Consistency Of Soft Butter And Your Skull Is Hard With Many Sharp Ridges.
5. Many Things Hurt The Brain And Many Things Help It.
6. Certain Systems In The Brain Tend To Do Certain Things And Problems In Those Systems Tend To Cause Specific Problems That Can Benefit From Specific Treatments.
7. Imaging Changes Everything.
8. All Psychiatric Illnesses Are Not Single Or Simple Disorders In The Brain. Each One Has Multiple Types That Require Unique Treatments.
9. Brain Aging Is Optional. Work To Boost Your Brain Reserve.
10. You Can Change Your Brain And Change Your Life.

There are several other malfunctioning neuroanatomical regions and circuits that can unfortunately lead to substance abuse. How do find out what may not be working so well? It is highly advisable to work closely with one's mental health professional to get answers. In addition, the Amen Clinics have questionnaires that can help guide one to a better understanding of their brain functioning. Finally, a SPECT scan would be great way to actually see how your brain is functioning. Such an assessment can give further guidance on how to best manage your brain.

Substance Abuse and Emotions

What causes the substance abuser to go on this this unrelenting reckless pursuit for drugs and alcohol? Where does this high drive originate? Where did they get such energy? There may be legal problems. There may be a family in disarray. There may be a loss of a job. Once the cravings kick in, consequences don't seem to matter.

Our media gives us countless examples of such wanton, sad foolhardiness. Numerous talented stars, athletes, and politicians had shortened lives. Their desire to use drugs trumped the unfortunate later consequences. Their quest to keep on using despite the "road kill" did not stop.

Why do these people keep on using? The answer to this question is quite complex and not fully solved. At some level, the brain is most likely looking to be in a more pleasurable state. With that goal in mind, there is at least one group of substance abusers who are trying to remove the impediments of negative feelings.6

Such individuals are at the extreme end of frequently feeling depressed, anxious, or

irritable. In their range of experiences in life, they have discovered that drugs give them the best chance of diminishing the intensity of these feelings. Such individuals have not been able to find that other, more natural internal skill sets to remove this "emotional sludge."

In addition to this group, there is another class of users who are those who are already fairly content with life. Rather than trying to free themselves from dredges of negativity, they are yearning to take their life to the "next level." These individuals often are trying to become more creative, experience more confidence, or take the concept of fun into a different stratosphere. Drugs become a shortcut to get to such a state. Rather than taking the time to find more natural means of experiencing joy, the substance abuser bypasses that route. It's easier to just "blow a line" or "take a mickey" to get to that state.

Research has expanded our understanding of what areas in the brain are associated with pleasure. Studies are indicating that a part of our midbrain, known as the nucleus accumbens, is one area responsible region. When this area of our brain is activated, a neurotransmitter, dopamine, is secreted to another midbrain structure, the ventral striatum. Subsequently, the ventral striatum is stimulated, resulting in an inner sense of joy and pleasure.

Illicit drugs are strong modulators that stimulate this pathway. At an elemental level, the strong urges to use are the brain's way of requesting more dopamine. If one can figure out other, alterior ways to get the brain to secrete dopamine, then the insatiable craving for drugs can decrease. Fortunately, we are beginning to find ways to get that "high" without the use of dangerous substances. Such luminary delight can be found in a number of much more constructive, health-promoting experiences.

Dopamine does more than create a sense of pleasure. It has also been found to strongly enhance motivation and desire to pursue a craved object.

Some conceptual activities can be potent promoters of secreting dopamine and experiencing joy include the following:

Sensation

This activity involves becoming aware and appreciating the many sensations (sight, sound, touch, smell, and taste) that we experience daily. Look for beautiful aesthetics, listen to great music, taste incredible good food, smell pleasing aromas, and feel the touch of a comfortable lounge chair. The more sensations the better. Many of the Cirque de Soleil shows take advantage of this concept.

Discovery

Discoveries include new experiences, insights, people, and places. Go on a hiking trail you have never taken. Take a trip to a foreign country. Go to a new restaurant opening in your community. Go on an internal journey and find something special about yourself.

Humor

Laughter is great medicine. Watch a comedian. See a great movie. Discover a new funny sitcom. Hang out with witty people.

Pride and Accomplishment

There is nothing greater than seeing the fruit of your hard work. These are powerfully personalized experiences. They make great stories to tell your friends, family, and colleagues. They will inspire you and inspire others.

Surprise

Our brains love positive surprises. The experience of something unexpected is very powerful. Don't wait for surprises to find you. The best way to seek them out is to expose yourself to new experiences. Also, try surprises on your friends. The experience can be just as riveting.

As you begin to experiment with these conceptualizations, it is important that you breathe life into them. Shape them. Mold them. Stretch them. Bend them. And by all means, have fun with them.

The key is to make these ideas more concrete and then take action to make these activities become alive. A concern is that these abstract concepts will remain just "words"--a bunch of theoretical intellectual jargon with nothing to back them up. If you remain idle, you won't experience the joy and freedom that can occur if you take the idea and turn it into real experiences. Get help if needed, but just don't let these conceptualizations become stale. They are powerful and do, indeed, get your brain to secrete the potent effects of dopamine.

Once you have toyed and flirted with these subjective constructs, there are other means to get a more natural high. Here are another 10 conceptualizations to start sculpting:

- **Fantasy**
- **Challenge**
- **Fellowship**
- **Expression**
- **Anticipation**
- **Gift Giving**
- **Possibility**
- **Thrill**
- **Triumph over Adversity**
- **Wonder**

Take these thought-enhancing words and let your imagination have some fun. Tinker with them. Take them apart. Analyze them. Expand them. Fight with them. Play with them. Then, take action! Go out and create some novel experiences to put your brain's pleasure center to work.

Finding Support

A common question from the substance abuser often deals with support systems: "Now that I have decided to be sober, are you inferring that I must go to Alcoholics

Anonymous? Narcotics Anonymous?" "Are you trying to somehow coax me to go to Rational Recovery?" "Are you suggesting that I can't do this on my own?"

Just a few decades ago, Alcoholics Anonymous was the primary support system used to encourage sobriety. Since then, there have been a number of new avenues created to stay free of drugs and alcohol. Each group has its strengths and inherent weaknesses.

Any of these groups, systems, organizations may or may not be a good fit for someone genuinely motivated to stay sober. Unlike the old days where one was reflexively told, "You need to go to an AA meeting," there are now numerous choices.

Whatever path that is chosen, there should be a common theme of questions that resonates in the decision making process.

Where can I learn to be honest to myself? How can I grow in humility?

Where can I find trust? Where can I find people with whom I can feel safe being vulnerable?

How can I find a great sponsor (mentor)?

How long has the sponsor been sober?

Do I respect the sponsor for the example that they are setting?

While creating this environment, it will be imperative to be able to safely start to look at the skeletons in your closet. Finding associations that will accept you as you are and lovingly challenge you to move forward will be tantamount. Groups that encourage feeling sorry for yourself, dating networks, and helplessness probably are not going to be the best fit. Hence, please choose wisely.

So as you start this new somewhat awkward lifestyle, I would suggest that you don't try to do it alone. Instead, look for friends, colleagues, church members, other sobriety seekers, who want that trust as well. Some of the biggest enemies we will ever face lie right between our two ears. As we bravely choose to look at them square in the face and defeat them, we need others that have skill sets to help us move beyond their decaying stench. You are going to need the internal strength, humility, and the outward support of others to guide you on this journey.

Summary

1. Substance abuse may often lead to unexpected negative surprises that are overlooked by the one addicted to illicit substances.
2. The frontal cortex of our brain plays a pivotal role in recognizing the dangers of substance abuse.
3. This important part of our brain is vulnerable and becomes damaged by the toxic effects of drugs and alcohol.
4. Neuroscience is beginning to demonstrate the nucleus accumbens, a neuroanatomical region of our brain that creates pleasure, as pivotal in substance abuse.
5. The number of incarcerated individuals with substance abuse disorders is dramatically elevated.
6. We need to humbly find other constructive activities with the active support of others to remain sober. By doing just this task, the rate of return to jails would markedly decrease.

Questions

1. Can you think of any substance abuse stories where consequences occurred that you never thought would happen? How did that make you feel? What were your subsequent thoughts about what transpired?
2. Please check out the following website on SPECT Scans, Substance Abuse and the Frontal Cortex: http://www.amenclinics.com/healthy-vs-unhealthy/ alcohol-drug-abuse/ Take a look at some of the scans of substance abusers versus those not abusing substances. For those of you who are substance abusers, what are your thoughts? How do you think your brain might look?
3. Hypothetically, let's pretend that you were just released from jail. You were told to find a place to stay and remain sober. If you could not remain sober, you would have to return to jail. What structures would you put into your life to stay away from drugs and alcohol?
4. Finding a great sponsor is crucial on your journey of abstinence. In addition to someone who has been living a dedicated life of sobriety, what other qualities would you like in a sponsor to help you live a constructive life?
5. Who are people you are going to need to stay away from to remain sober?

6. Who are people you are going to want to be around to remain abstinent?

7. Make a plan to see those people you need to be around at least once per day.

8. There are lots of choices of finding support groups. What steps are you going to take to find a great group for you? How will you know if the group is a good fit?

9. There were 15 areas where one can find pleasure to activate the nucleus accumbens. Pick an area and write down 20 potential activities that encompass that theme (it seems like a lot but the ideas usually get better as you persist).

10. Pick an activity that you can reasonably do as well as afford, and go for it! What was it like? How much fun (or not fun) did you have?

11. If you really liked the activity, could you build mastery from it (remember that mastery increases self-esteem)? If so, how would you do it?

12. Try doing a brainstorming session at one of your support groups and see what pleasurable activities they can come up with from question 9. How was the experience? Did you find the list of activities increasing at a higher rate?

13. How might you get to know your brain better and understand its irrational drive for illicit substances?

14. Look in a local newspaper or magazine. Find five activities that have nothing to do with drugs or alcohol. Then, go to one of the events. How was it? Did you have fun? Did you not have fun? What will you do in the future (whether you had fun or didn't have fun)?

15. Given your history, honestly answer how much structure you are going to need to remain abstinent? Who in your life can hold you to that level of commitment?

NOTES

CHAPTER 4

Growing

I t was April 1987. There was a lot going on in the world. The Stock Market was getting closer to its largest crash since the Great Depression. Texaco, the mega-sized corporation, filed for bankruptcy. Boxer Sugar Ray Leonard came out of retirement and defeated the youthful Marvin Hagler. Basketball great Michael Jordan scored 3,000 points in one season. The Vietnam War film "Platoon" won an Oscar. "The Great One" Wayne Gretzky scored seven goals in one game. Singer Paul Simon won a Grammy. Homer Simpson made his debut on television. Emmy Award- winning "Hill Street Blues" came to an end. The world was moving and changing fast.

During that spring in a small studio in West Hollywood, California, co-producers Michael Jackson and Quincy Jones were working on Michael's new album, "Bad," scheduled to come out at the end of the summer. It had been five years since the cosmic selling "Thriller" left audiences spellbound. It was hoped that this new release would soar to greater heights on the billboard charts.

There was one problem. Nine of the ten songs for the album had been written and produced. One final tune was needed. Whatever song was chosen, it would have to embody rhythm, power, and energy. To solve this dilemma, Jones assigned a group of songwriters to come up with the last hit. Shortly after the announcement, pop artists Siedah Garett and Glen Ballard sat down, played with some chords, toyed with some lyrics, and in less than 48 hours wrote one of the most high-impact pop songs of the 20th century.

Not knowing if Michael would ever get to hear the song, Garett called Jones immediately after it was complete. Excited about the potential for this to be a real hit, Garett communicated her sense of urgency to her boss. "Just drop it off Monday at the office," Jones busily told Garett. Boldly, Garett did not think this one could wait.

"No, I am going to drop this song personally off at your home," she retorted. A bit annoyed, Jones gruffly growled, "Fine, just drop it off at my home."

A few hours later, Garrett raced up to Jones home. Her arrival could not have been better timed. It turned out that her boss, Jones, was having a big corporate executive meeting in the living room. A bit peeved, Jones took the cassette tape from Garrett, swiftly carted her to the front door, and rumbled that he would listen later.

Knowing that her grand entry had been annoying, Garrett did not think she would hear back from Jones until at least Monday. Three hours after her departure, Jones surprisingly called Garrett back. "Sideah, this has got to be the best song I have heard in the last 10 years." Trying to contain her excitement, Jones then let out the cautionary (oh no) "BUT...it still has to be approved by Michael."

Over the years, Jackson had written the material for his songs himself. He did not like to use the artistry of others fearing it would take away from his epic "King of Pop" Style. The likelihood of this song ever getting past Jackson were extremely low...and Garrett knew it.

Three days later, Garrett received another "stunner" call from Jones. "Sideah, you aren't going to believe this. Michael is recording your song right now for 'Bad.' He is using your song for his album. I can't even believe it," Jones commented. Garrett and Ballard had done the unthinkable, they had created a song that had penetrated both the heart and mind of Jackson's creativity. Jackson was a voice to the "eyes and ears of the entire planet." The essence of the song had to be of legendary epic power to ever have gotten this far.

This song proved to live up to all expectations. It peaked at Number One in January 1998 becoming the fourth such song on the album to hit that level. It hit the BillBoard Top 100 for two weeks. The song ended all his concerts; it captured a large part of humanitarian efforts; and, it was the "final goodbye" played at his memorial in 2009.

It captivated leaders of the world; it inspired his young listeners; it was a unique blend of taking contemporary "cool" and delivering a time-honored universal message. And, the beauty is that the song continues to transcend its age having over 1.3 million downloads on iTunes following Jackson's death.

So what is this song? What message did it send? What type of tune could remain so ageless and trendy and be popular today? The song is… "Man in the Mirror." It is a message about accountability, personal development, and the impact we can all make, if we just decide to look at one person, ourselves: "The Man in the Mirror."

For those who have never seen the original music video, it is definitely worthwhile watching (http://www.youtube.com/watch?v=PivWY9wn5ps). It is one of the only Jackson visual graphic presentations that does not contain any of his mesmerizing choreography. No dancing, no instruments, no Jackson Instead, the video contains moving portrayals of hunger, homelessness, racism, war, and the world leaders who have pushed the world forward.

After watching the video, there is one other element to this "modern day pop scripture that gives it even more impact. During the last 90 seconds of this song, there is mainly rhythmic instrumentation, minimal vocalization, and a choir humming in the background. A music critic could innocently misinterpret this part of the song as dragging on a bit too long. It's repetitious, redundant, and monotonous. It seems like the song, well, just needs to come to an end.

Should you be of that similar belief, a strong suggestion would be to watch this song performed at the 1988 Grammy Awards (https://www.youtube.com/watch?v=ljpl0neGk2Q). While the choir is singing during those last 90 seconds, Jackson is "getting down," showing off his eye-catching, sensationalized dance moves. However, if one were to

Jackson Producer Quincy Jones

take a slightly closer look, there is actually something much deeper and very special going on.

Jackson "ain't just strutting his stuff." Instead, he is actually miming what an ordinary human goes through when they make a decision to change. There's heartache; there's joy; there's anguish; there's exhilaration; there's pain; and there's celebration.

In a mere 90 seconds, Jackson uses his cultural genius to show what we all go through when we make that decision to transcend our own personal misgivings and make a difference. As we begin to work on personal development, you keep this video closely at your side. You will connect; you will engage; and you will be moved to keep moving forward.

Despite some of the past controversy regarding Jackson, this song has left all of us with something very special. We miss you, Michael.

Why Is Personal Development Important?

So what makes the practice of personal development so important? As many of you leave the legal system, you are going to have to deal with a lot of barriers. Because of your past convictions, people are going to be less likely to hire you. Finding a safe place to stay will be a challenge. Society, in general, will be less willing to trust you. Many will view you as a second-class citizen. And, these people won't be so willing to give you a second chance. This may seem harsh. It may seem cruel. It may seem unfair. Whether one agrees with these biases or not, it is a poignant reality.

This unpleasant fact gives you much less control over your life. It's also important to remember these opinions will not change overnight. As difficult as this situation can be, the only real tactic to cope is to accept it. Realize that it is going to take time for people to trust you. You can't change people's opinions and biases. You can only ride the ebbs and flows of optimism and despair as your journey out of jail continues.

Although you cannot control others' predetermined beliefs, you can certainly help influence them. This is where the notion of personal development plays such a pivotal role. Constructive individualized growth can deliver great returns so long as you take the time to nurture it every day.

Steve Farber, a renowned leadership author, describes this discipline as "expanding yourself." Farber mentions that the beauty in this discipline is that there is no floor or ceiling effect. One can always work at being better. "No matter how smart, how focused, how confident, how team oriented, how stable you see yourself, there is always an opportunity to get better." You can always twist, turn, bend, and shake to become better.1

And it is this skill that no one can control; no one command; no one can manipulate; no one can use power...except for you. So take advantage of this reality. Become the change that you want the world to see.

Some other important features about personal development are that it builds mental tenacity and defeats laziness. For many, it can become very easy to live a self-justified lifestyle of voluntary victimization. "My mom didn't encourage me enough." "My father left when I was age five." "All the kids in elementary school teased me." "I am too fat." "I am too skinny." "I flunked math." "I did not pass high school." So what do we do in these "woe is me" instances? We whine. We complain. We seethe. We lay on the couch all day. We watch television learning how we deserve to be self-entitled.

So what is the end result of our pity party? We end up feeling good knowing that we were somehow wronged in life. We righteously justify our pitiful existence. We religiously sanctify our need not to change. Internally, we feel victoriously vindicated. Externally though, we get torn to pieces. Ripped, shredded, and humiliated.

Come on gang, let's move on and stop crying in our "voluntary victim" handkerchiefs. Let's get off our "adult baby" diapers and put on some real underwear. Let's stop eating baby food and eat some real, real, tangible, growth-promoting, vibrant material that makes us into respectable adults. This is mental laziness at its best. Personal development leads us out of that mentality.

Finally, personal development gives us hope and power. There are going to be days ahead that are going to be tough. One of the hardest parts of this process is doing the right stuff and then being hit by an unexpected surprise.

In my office, one of my patients recently released from jail had been making incredible strides in moving on and moving forward. He saw tangible results from his hard efforts. He was becoming more confident. His belief in himself was expanding. Then, the sudden unexpected "earthquake" hit. My patient received a phone call from an ex-girlfriend. Things were going so well for the patient that he subconsciously thought that the call was going to be another "blessing from above" for his hard efforts.

As they started talking, joking, laughing, and playing off each other's unique quirks, my patient began to think his ex was calling to get back together. Silently he thought, "Wow! This hard work really pays off. I never dreamed in my life that she would come back." In the midst of their rekin-dling joyous memories, the unexpected IED went off. The ex-girlfriend took a sudden quick spin in the conversation, letting my patient know that she was engaged to be married. Boom! Explosion set off! Who saw that coming?

Disappointment could not even begin to describe the inner anguish of my patient. He was blind-sided. He was taken for a loop. He sensed he was tricked.

Then, all the well-ingrained circuitry of my patient's default mode network began to display its ugly head. "What's the purpose of me working so hard to be better?" "Nothing ever changes." "This sucks." "I am pissed." "I quit."

One of the most painful experiences any of us can feel is when our expectations are not met. This disconcerting experience is even worse when we don't see it coming. Wham! It feels like you have been "sucker punched." Someone took the wind right out of you. The only way to protect yourself, you think, is to return to old patterns.

Please don't fall back. That is the last thing you want to do. Personal development will give you the hope and courage to move beyond the event. In reality, the perceived victim is moving beyond their current circumstances to bigger and better things. They just have enough faith to know that the short-term pain will lead to long-term gain. You just have to stay committed to the process of personal development.

Although it was hard to see in the moment, my patient was actually moving beyond his ex-girlfriend to a healthier and more fulfilling relationship. During the chaos, turmoil, and pandemonium of the "verbal bomb" going off, it was hard for my patient to see (and believe) that he was moving on to greener pastures.

The discipline of personal development is a process that arms you with the necessary tools of hope, courage, and trust to keep moving forward. We cannot control the uncertainty of the future. What we can do is consciously, purposefully, and creatively develop an internal environment that will bring the highest dividends one year, two years, five years, and 10 years down the road.

Personal development is the daily investment of hope and courage to deliver the optimum return not on your finances, but your life! The beauty of this process is that it's free and that you can reap quick rewards so long as you create the correct system to take advantage of its power.

Create an Environment of Personal Development

How do you develop this structure of constant improvement? For those of you who don't yet have a daily system created, there are two routes that you can choose to use separately or in combination. The first system, The Traditional System, is one that I have personally used for years. The second system involves the use of guided personalized meditation.

The Traditional System
A. Pick an Area to Grow

First, just find an area where you genuinely want to grow. That endeavor should not be difficult, right? Just pick something. It should be simple. It should not be complicated. It should be relatively easy.

For some, the making of a sound choice of where to grow might be just that easy. The process of choosing can be enlightening, encouraging, and fun. For others, though, this process may be cumbersome and confusing. It can generate fear and anxiety. Frustration, uncertainty, and lack of guidance can bring this process to a screeching halt.

For those of you that fit into this latter category, let it be known that there are a number of helpful ways to get started. Most important, you are going to want to find an area that is relevant to your situation. Don't be arbitrary. Don't be nonchalant. Pick an area that has some "meat and bone" to it. For example, if you are looking for a job, you might want to find some material on how to present well on a job interview. If you have struggled with anger over the years, there is a vast amount of material on how to control your anger. For those who are not understanding of their significant other's needs, you might want to explore ways to be more empathic.

Put some thought into it. Be reflective. Make your brain work a bit. Then if you still can't find a meaningful area, ask for some help from others. Ask your spouse; go see your pastor; call a friend; talk to your parole officer. Those who know you best will be likely to steer you in the right direction to get the biggest bang for your time investment.

If you need to ask others for help, this is not a time to see yourself as a weak or inferior human being. In actuality, you are being very assertive and strong. Research is now indicating that individuals with poor frontal lobe-striatal connectivity have a higher association of demonstrating "Environmental Dependency." Such brains find it more difficult to take initiative and be flexible with their choices. In other words, these brains find it hard to make a decision and you need constructive assistance from others.[2]

As you get to understand your brain, you want to utilize behaviors that allow your brain to work at its highest capacity. For those with frontal lobe-striatal connectivity problems, you are actually doing your central nervous system a favor.

When asking others for guidance, how do you know if you have hit a great area to strive on improving? Some might be fortunate enough to get an "ah-ah" experience. "That's it!" "Now, I know!" "This idea really hits home."

Although these moments contain a high emotional punch, they are not the most common.

For those who don't experience "Eureka!," it is advisable to pick one of three pertinent areas and move forward. Just take a risk and start. Plunge in deeply and see what happens. If you start getting some great feedback and/or incredible results, you will know that you are on an important pathway. In contrast, if you sense you are not moving forward, not getting meaningful feedback (please note that negative feedback is not the same as meaningful feedback), or if you are not motivated, don't stop just yet.

Instead, make a commitment to work hard at your chosen area for another two weeks. Give it your best shot. Be deliberate. Be intentional. Be committed. Just don't quit during that two week period. Then, at the end of that time if you feel the same way, pick another area to personally develop.

B. Find Resources

Resources are any type of information that help you improve on the area that you want to focus. Such information may be traditionally found in books, either purchased or loaned from a library, magazines, newspapers, and the Internet.

If you do not like to read, there are an abundance of audio resources available. Of note, there are a number of audio books found on CDs or that can downloaded to be played on a smartphone or MP3 player. Moreover, there are fantastic podcasts on the Internet, many of which are free of charge.

In addition to great listening material, there are fantastic video presentations streamlined on the online. Websites such as YouTube have an endless array of hot information topics. At their website, all one needs to do is type in a topic of interest and zap! You will have huge numbers of videos to choose of your liking. Another website that you might want to check out is the TED Conferences (www.ted.com). This site is comprised of some of the planet's greatest leaders talking about their areas of expertise. These trending teachers typically give 20-minute presentations that prompt the viewer to explore these areas in greater depth.

If you really want to take this research to the next level, consider Google searching experts, companies, movies, and songs that pertain to your interest. The Internet's ability to effectively deliver information has made it much easier to delve deeply into the area you are studying. Two decades ago, one would have needed to make numerous trips to a public library, government institutions, and pertinent organizations. Now, you can sit alone with your computer, access much of this information online, and not have to travel at all.

Because information is so much more available, another important skill set is important to develop. It used to be that those who memorized and regurgitated information (i.e. those with better grades in school) were the most likely to succeed. This trend is starting to change.

Computers do a much better job of saving and retrieving information than the human brain. With a couple types on a keyboard, one can pull up the 50 state capitals, the 11 causes of high blood pressure, or the five major characters in Hamlet in seconds.

As efficient as computers are, they still cannot do a very important human task in our learning process. Computers don't ask great questions. They lack the creativity, insight, and ingenuity to perform this feat.

How does this reality affect you on your journey of self-improvement? You are going to need to learn to ask great questions! "Who are the top five experts in my area of interest? How can I find out about them? How can I learn from them?" What are barriers that stop me from growing in my area? How can I identify them? How can I get past them? Who are people that have been where I am now that succeeded? What can I learn from them? Can I reach them? Should I call them personally?"

The 21st century will be known for those who ask the best questions, accumulate great information, and then take committed action to move forward. You have a significant benefit from those in past decades. Take advantage of this opportunity and advance.

C. Process the Material You Are Studying

Take notes, underline, write comments, jot down questions, make summaries, doodle, draw, and circle those thoughts that seem most important. Then go back and review your scribbles. Such activity makes it easier to stay engaged when you are learning. Moreover, it helps prioritize what is important to you. Finally, it saves a good chunk of time having to scrub back through voluminous amounts of material. Make it easier on yourself by using this efficient shortcut.

D. Journal

Years ago, I had the privilege to go over to John Maxwell's home in Atlanta. For those of you who have not heard of Maxwell, he is a well-known leadership author who has written several "New York Times" best-selling books. While in his home office, Maxwell made a comment that I have valued to this day. The concept was simple, yet so profound. Maxwell said to me, "One of the most important things you do to advance in life is value your thoughts. Whatever you are thinking, take treasure of it."

That was interesting. For many years, I was primarily trying to value my emotions. I wanted to be happy. I worked on having a good attitude. At an early age, I sought out ways to control a horrible temper. I thought emotions were important, not thoughts.

Many of you may experience that your thoughts are "just there" marinating in a sea of "non-importance." They exist, spiritless, barely alive, passively indifferent, close to being flat-lined. If you are in such a predicament, what are you supposed to do to genuinely value your thoughts? (That's where I was.)

Sulking in any dilemma is not a great place to stay. If you truly don't value your thinking, then the next best thing that you can do is value your apathy and passive indifference about your perceptions. Take heed that you just do not find much worthwhile. Come to accept your spiritlessness. Choose to embrace your boring lassitude.

As strange as it might sound, acknowledging this unpleasant reality begins to kindle a deeper awareness of your need to find worth in your thinking. Over time, you begin to discover ways to think creatively and appreciate the hidden value of the unique flashing ideas within you.

If you are already practicing this habit, fantastic. Keep up the good work. But for those of you who have not given yourself this opportunity, really take the time to value your thoughts. You don't necessarily have to love how you currently think. Just start to value the chasm of where you currently are with your thinking and where you eventually want to be. This is where the magic starts to happen.

Next, start to journal down your thoughts; those that are not valued, undervalued, and genuinely valued. A whole book could be written just on how to use journaling to spark new ideas, discover hidden talents, and uncover powerful beliefs. Without going into such detail here are some questions you can use after you study a topic to get your brain moving forward.

- What one idea did I find important in what I learned?
- Was there a time in my life when I could relate to that idea? If so, when was it?
- If I have not experienced this idea, how could I expand this idea in my life?
- Who exemplifies this idea well? What makes them special?
- What emotions come up when I think of this idea?
- If I am indifferent about the idea, how might I try to make it more real to me?

- What results might I experience if I practice this idea?
- What emotions come up if I were to practice this idea? How do I deal with those emotions?
- How can I challenge myself today with this idea?
- What are 20 ideas for how I could experience the idea today (yes, 20; the best ideas usually come at the end of the list).

These questions are only a start. There are myriad of other questions to get your brain activated. As you grow in this area, you will discover other unique questions to ignite your brain to discover the greater powers within yourself.

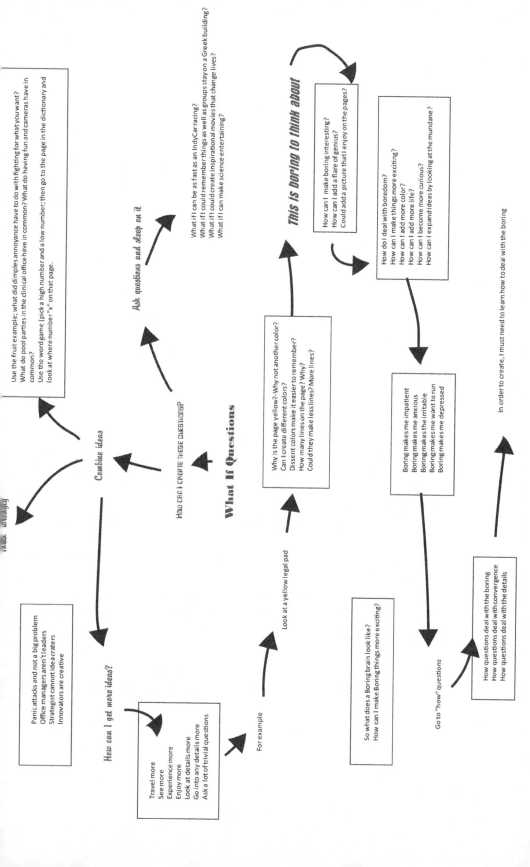

Phase steady

Combine ideas

Use the fruit example; what did dimples annoyance have to do with fighting for what you want? What do pool parties in the clinical office have in common? What do having fun and cameras have in common?

Use the word game (pick a high number and a low number; then go to the page in the dictionary and look at where number "x" on that page.

Ask questions and sleep on it

What if I can be as fast as an IndyCar racing?
What if I could remember things as well as groups stay on a Greek building?
What if I could create inspirational movies that change lives?
What if I can make science entertaining?

HOW CAN I CREATE THESE QUESTIONS?

What If Questions

This is boring to think about

How can I make boring interesting?
How can I add a flare of genius?
Could add a picture that I enjoy on the pages?

How do I deal with boredom?
How can I make things more exciting?
How can I add more color?
How can I add more life?
How can I become more curious?
How can I expand ideas by looking at the mundane?

Why is the page yellow? Why not another color?
Can I create different colors?
Dissent colors make it easier to remember?
How many lines on the page? Why?
Could they make less lines? More lines?

Boring makes me impatient
Boring makes me anxious
Boring makes the irritable
Boring makes me want to run
Boring makes me depressed

In order to create, I must need to learn how to deal with the boring

How can I get more ideas?

Panic attacks and not a big problem
Office managers aren't leaders
Strategist cannot create idea craters
Innovators are creative

Travel more
See more
Experience more
Enjoy more
Look at details more
Go into any details more
Ask a lot of trivial questions

Look at a yellow legal pad

For example

So what does a Boring brain look like?
How can I make Boring things more exciting?

Go to "how" questions

How questions deal with the boring
How questions deal with convergence
How questions deal with the details

Meditation

Another great way to begin to develop a larger entourage of positive emotional experiences is by meditating. Meditation is the disciplined practice of training the mind to sharpen its awareness of consciousness, particularly on positive states. It is used to as a means to effortlessly experience the powerful benefits of peace, patience, love, forgiveness, compassion and wonder. Moreover, meditation can be used to self-regulate more unpleasant states such as anger, depression, despair, rage, and anxiety.

Once the techniques of meditation are understood and practiced, its profound positive effects can be experienced very quickly. In addition, using these practices is easy in many different environments without others even being aware. Such practices become valuable tools in learning how to cope with the daily stresses of life.

How do you practice meditation? Although there are many methods to choose, the techniques utilized by author John Selby are practical, easy to use, and can be done in numerous settings. To begin, start by reading one line each time you inhale.

> Say to yourself, "I feel the air blowing in and out of my nose."
>
> Say to yourself, "I also feel the movements in my chest and my belly as I breathe."
>
> Say to yourself, "I'm also aware of the feelings in my heart."
>
> Say to yourself, "I let go of bad feelings and choose to feel good," or "I give myself permission to feel good.
>
> Say to yourself, "My mind is quiet, my emotions calm (let go of your worries)."
>
> Say to yourself, "I honor and respect the person I am meeting with (do not be judgmental)."
>
> Say to yourself, "I feel good toward my own self (stop self-sabotage)."
>
> Say to yourself, "I open my heart to receive friendship and enjoy good feelings with this person."[3]

When you get to the bottom affirmation, go back to the top and repeat the exercise. The exercise readily aids you to live in the present free from the internal stress, frustration, and anxiety.

Another tremendous type of meditation is known as "Integrative Awareness" or FOCAR. Dr. Marcelo Urban, from Brazil, has developed a very powerful meditation technique that he has been using to work with prisoners in Brazil. His revolutionary breakthrough system has been teaching those with fear, anger, hate, disgust,

distrust, and other damaging emotions to use their own inner brain circuitry to dissolve these emotions. The intensity, power, and negativity of these damaging feelings quickly diminishes by using the forces of one's own inner ability to heal.

Moreover, the practice of FOCAR naturally replaces loathsome, abhorred emotions with those that are incredibly powerful and part of your true essence. As hate, envy, rage, depression, anxiety, etc. dissipate, FOCAR subtly guides the brain to its more natural pleasant state. In this condition, the brain brings forth the experiences of peace, joy, bliss, love, and unconditional acceptance. Often, the meditator is tearfully surprised to discover that these feelings are alive and spontaneously present himself or herself.

Dr Marcelo Urban; Founder of the FOCAR Technique

By using this technique, Dr. Urban and his team have seen a profound decrease in the number of prisoners returning back to jail. The technique is simple, easy to use, and doesn't cost a cent! Once someone masters the skills of FOCAR, they can be used at any time: morning, noon, or night to quickly dissipate the power of violent negative feelings.

Summary

1. No one has control over how others view our reputation and personhood, only we do. We need to accept this reality.
2. We do have control over how we develop ourselves. Personal development is very important to move to next levels in our life.
3. We need to start by looking at the "Man in the Mirror" to profoundly change.

4. Personal development will have its ebbs and flows. In downtimes, consider watching Michael Jackson's 1988 Grammy Awards performance of "Man in the Mirror." You will connect, be inspired, and be given hope.
5. Practice the discipline of personal development daily.
6. Learn to Value Your Thoughts!
7. Learn to journal and meditate to improve yourself.

Questions

1. What opportunities in the past, if any, have you been exposed to personal growth? What was the experience like? How might you make the experience even more enriching?
2. Where are some areas in which you would actually like to grow?
3. If you are not sure where you would want to personally grow, who could you ask for some assistance? Would you be willing to ask them for help? If not, what are the barriers holding you back?
4. What would be the advantages of personal growth in your life?
5. If you decide you want to start developing, do you think you could really pull it off? What might be some barriers that you experience? How can you strategically confront them?
6. What type of thoughts and feelings arise when you think of journaling?
7. What might be some ways to make sure that journaling is an actively engaging experience?
8. What if journaling becomes boring or you feel stagnated with that process? Who could you talk with to enliven the experience?
9. What are the advantages and disadvantages of meditation? How might you make the advantages become greater than the disadvantages?
10. Who are well-recognized people that meditate? What do they say about its effects on their lives?
11. Who might help you progress forward to stay focused on personal development? How could you ask them to be your accountability partner?
12. What time of day works best for you to work on improving yourself? Where do you practice this discipline? How long do you practice? How many days do you commit to practicing?

13. Would this be an activity that you would like to put on your daily schedule? If so, what time of day and what materials are you going to use (tapes, books, Internet, articles)?

14. How long are you going to practice that attribute that you choose to change? What will be the next area you work on? (Remember, our brains like to know what is coming next.)

15. When we work on changing ourselves, it can be the best and worst of times. How are we going to cope when making transformations is hard? What about if we have a great success? How can you constructively celebrate?

16. Watch Michael Jackson's music video, "Man in the Mirror." What types of emotions did it bring up for you? How did it help define your perception of change?

NOTES

CHAPTER 5

Mentoring

At 16 years old, Jovan Hoover had more on her plate than she could chew. Already taking care of a baby girl, Hoover needed to drop out of high school to take care of her little boy. Young, uneducated, and overwhelmed, Hoover did not know if her future could turn out favorably. There were a number of opportunities that she wanted to pursue. However, those options suddenly narrowed by having to take care of a toddler.

Hoover wanted to graduate from high school. She dreamed of someday going to college. Her hopes were to be a great example for her son and provide solely for his well-being. How was she going to do that without any funds? Where would she find the time to commit to getting a GED? Then, a college degree? Come on, let's be realistic.

Clearly, the circumstances were not in Hoover's favor. If statistics would bear themselves out, there would be minimal chance that she would be able to pursue the lifestyle that she so desired. More than likely, food stamps, welfare, and supported housing would become her best friends.

Despite the odds, Hoover was determined to achieve her dreams. The storm of frequent negative comments were not going to become the denigrating recipe for sloth, victimization, and hopelessness. Somehow, some way, Hoover was going to find some other ingredients that would make a nutritious meal of accountability, belief, and inspiration.

Hoover recognized that she would need to focus upon several areas to reach her goals. Determination and perseverance would have to become more of her character. Equally important, Hoover keenly identified the essential need to be surrounded by one or two encouraging people to develop these traits.

Subsequently, Hoover discovered a local volunteer group, YouthBuild, which offered guidance and direction. YouthBuild is a national nonprofit organization that serves troubled, unemployed young adults, ages 16-24, who are typically high school dropouts. This program teaches leadership skills that make the young adults more employable once they are done with the program.

Instruction, coaching, and guidance are given while the students are building homes for the underserved. When not out hammering nails, hanging sheetrock, or painting drywall, the students are given formal classroom instruction to obtaining their General Equivalence Diploma (GED). This on-site mentoring approach provides training on how to be servant leaders for their families, their neighborhoods, and themselves. The student-leader relationships help train accountability, self-direction, and healthy self-esteem. Subsequently, active trainees begin to have increased belief, no longer seeing themselves as a burden; but instead, a resource to be tapped. Once completed, the graduate obtains his/her GED, placement in jobs, and the potential to go to college.

Hoover took full advantage of the mentoring program. Not only did she obtain her GED, she went on to receive her bachelor's degree from Morgan State University majoring in marketing and minoring in accounting. With that degree, Hoover boldly demonstrated that you could beat the odds with the support from others. In her words, "I had the support of Dorothy Stoneman (The Founder of Youth Build) 110 percent and the support of my family. That was just basically it. I knew I had someone I could pretty much call on. Youth Build was definitely there along with the support of my family."[1]

Hoover's support network proved invaluable during times of duress. On one occasion, Hoover almost had to drop out of school after being unexpectedly told that room and board would no longer be provided. During this time, Hoover felt like "just giving up." It was discouraging to be so committed and then be surprisingly bombarded by unforeseen events. Rather than quit, Hoover reached out to her mentor, Dorothy Stoneman, who made some calls and helped her find suitable housing. Looking back, Hoover recognized the invaluable need to have this level of support. Unplanned events can and will occur. Without the guidance, encouragement, and prodding from others, it would be all too easy to throw in the towel.

Mentoring

A mentor is a person who unconditionally values another person while imparting his/ her wisdom and knowledge to guide them. This person helps the "mentored" identify what they are trying to achieve in life and holds them respectfully accountable to

attain it. Frequent meetings, relationship building, and constant feedback become powerful instruments to move the "mentored" in a positive direction.

Mentors can come in all shapes and sizes; young, old, tall, short, quiet, loud, listeners, and motivators. They can be found in many places, schools, churches, synagogues, offices, locker rooms, coffee shops, restaurants, cafeterias, clothing stores, computer shops…they are everywhere! The challenge is discovering them and then being bold enough to ask one of them to be a mentor.

For some, this may seem a bit awkward. It may create some "angst." It might make you slightly uncomfortable. It won't though, physically harm you to let someone know that, first, you really admire the example they set and then ask if they would mind being your mentor for a few months. In order for you to move on in life, you are going to need to have a mentor!

What qualities make a great mentor? Here is a list of helpful qualities:

They want to see you succeed.
They challenge you to be more curious and inquisitive.
They motivate you.
They inspire you.
They don't lessen your dreams.
They help you believe in yourself.
They boldly confront you when your actions are not in harmony with your established purpose.

In addition to this list, there is one other important attribute about the mentor. The mentor is credible with an established track record of constructive results. A mentor may be someone who has been teaching anger management classes for several years with lots of success stories to back them up. They are not someone who has just completed a domestic violence workshop following a conviction of an assault. A mentor may be an individual who has been sober for several years sincerely seeing and teaching the benefits of a drug-free life. It is not an individual who completed a residential program a month ago that you met at a support meeting. A mentor could be a small business owner who has hired several employees over the past decade at his/her company. They are not someone who recently found a job after being unemployed for the past year.

As overly simplistic as these examples may sound, it is amazing how many people submit to leadership that does not have legitimate credibility. Subsequently, those being mentored become disenchanted when their mentors fail. It is disappointing; it is heartbreaking; it is demoralizing. So painful for some that they lose hope and return to less constructive behaviors.

Please don't fall into this trap. Respect yourself enough to say "no" to these well-meaning, but not yet credible people. You deserve better. You are going to need people who have been through the "hurricanes of Katrina," you are going to need guidance by those who felt the shakings of the "earthquakes of California," and you are going to need the tranquility of those who have seen the "tornadoes of the great plains." These mentors have been there, seen it, tasted it, and felt it. They did not break. Instead, they broke records. Those are the kind of mentors that you are going to need in your life.

More importantly, you deserve that kind of mentor. Do not shortchange yourself.

Why are Mentors so Important?

As you enter back into the mainstream of society, it is not always going to be easy. Life can and will (guaranteed!) throw "curveballs" at you. There will be the unexpected "blitzes" of new bills to pay. There will be the unpleasant "interceptions" of others trying to steal your new found self-belief. There are going to be the "10-yard holding penalties" because you impulsively became angry at work and lost a job. A mentor is going to support you during these painful times.

The mentor's very presence becomes the Kevlar® vest of hope. Bullets come; bullets go. Mistakes come; mistakes go. Criticism comes; criticism goes. A mentor comes; a mentor stays!

The very foundation of a permanent figure helps our brains function at a higher capacity. The concept of "attachment" has become one of important significance in the field of brain physiology. Epidemiologically, 40 percent (this is no small number!)

of the population has been raised in homes with insecure attachments. Such individuals are more prone to become more anxious, more irritable, more angry, and more willing to quit when life gets tough. One significant purpose of a mentor is to help your brain's functionality be with those other 60 percent who were raised with secure attachments. Such individuals are typically more emotionally stable, optimistic, and able to persevere through the hard times. The mentor serves as a "surrogate caregiver" to help our brain function at a higher capacity.

In addition to this crucial role, the mentor is also there to impart wisdom on essential "life skill sets" when you will need guidance. Pertinent topics such as goal setting, leadership, mental stamina, anger management, and accountability are taught through the power of the relationship.

Additionally, the person being mentored will offer more concrete counsel on how to find suitable housing; how to find a secure, permanent job; how to open a bank account and pay your bills on time. In essence, the mentor becomes a living,

breathing, moving "Home Depot ™ Instruction Manual" on how to remodel your brain's interior.

As enticing as this 'home renovation" concept may sound, there is one caveat. You are most likely going to be working with a person who has different interior design preferences. If you are used to having a kitchen with linoleum floors, your mentor might be used to walking on travertine marble. If you are used to watching television on a 30-inch flat screen, your mentor may be viewing shows on a monitor twice that size, with 3D capacity, and Surround Sound speakers. If you are used to taking a shower in a tub with plastic curtains, your mentor may be refreshingly cleaning in a walk-in shower with glass walls, Italian marble, and brass fixtures.

So what does this gibberish exactly mean? Your mentor's guidance will be taking you into a different world. That experience is going to cognitively seem foreign or strange to your brain. Emotionally, the feelings surrounding the event could mistakenly seem uncomfortable or even "dark." Darkness correlates with anxiety, frustration, tension, irritability, sluggishness, apathy, detachment, disengagement, or fear. Depending on your brain's physiology and circuitry, you could feel some, all, or a mixture of these feelings.

In order to move through this transition, it is going to be imperative that you remain humble through the experiences. Humility, in this context, does not mean being passive, meek, or blindly obedient. Instead, humility means that you are honest about your feelings and begin to constructively deal with them. We don't run and avoid. We don't attack our mentor's suggestions. We become curious; we become inquisitive; we become mindful. Foundationally, we get more intimately acquainted with ourselves and our brain such that we can move forward in the directions we unconsciously need and desperately desire.

We don't run from the darkness. We shine light on it. We use our mentors and such tools as journaling, meditating, and active thinking to embark on the "epic journey."

My nephew, Danny, is a great example of this experience. Danny grew up in Minnesota and just graduated from high school. Throughout most of his childhood and adolescent years, Danny was "labeled" as different from other students and even family members. Despite the extreme, cold winters, Minnesota is an active community where many young boys are involved in playing the popular sports of football, baseball, and ice hockey.

Danny, instead, chose not to play any of these sports. He became actively involved in the theater and performing arts at his local high school. Because of his connections, Danny dressed differently than most of the rest of the Midwestern culture. Because of a more conservative mindset, Danny was often classified as being a bit "out there."

Fortunately, Danny's father and mother saw things differently. Rather than judging him as being "less of a man," they saw their son as a passionate teen wanting to develop his personal interests. When others criticized, these parents encouraged. While others laughed, these parents taught Danny to laugh at them. While others shook their heads, his parents taught Danny that he would be shaking heads in the future.

Danny just graduated from high school. He won't be getting a hockey scholarship at a Division I or Division II School in Minnesota. He won't be going to a Midwestern college and getting a degree in business. He won't be hanging out at the sports bars watching the Vikings.

Instead, Danny will take his passion to a whole other level. Danny got accepted at the prestigious New York University School of Performing Arts. In order to be enrolled, Danny had to go sing and perform live at this well-respected institute competing with hungry actresses/actors throughout the world. Roughly four weeks after Danny did his audition, he received a letter from New York University stating that he had been accepted.

For 18 years, Danny felt the darkness of feeling "less than others," receiving unfair criticism, and being labeled as different. Throughout his childhood and adolescence, Danny painfully experienced the harsh "rubber-stamping" that would make many want to quit. Throughout his senior high school days, Danny endured the sarcasm and humiliation while being encouragingly prodded by his mentors, Mom and Dad.

Danny has a very positive future ahead of himself. He has gone through some significant darkness and now will see some glowing light, being around a community of people who understand the power of performing arts.

Social Support

In addition to finding a great mentor, it will be equally important to surround yourself with a social network of people who will be supportive of your new endeavors. That environment becomes a constant motivator. It pushes you. It inspires you. It excites you. Between those times you meet with your mentor, it will be imperative that you find a group of friends who equally prod you forward.

For some, you may doubt the importance of developing a supportive network around you. "Why do I need friends? I am strong enough to do this on my own." Furthermore, the very thought of finding new friends is hard work. "Why do I want to replace my past friends? They are fun. Why would I want to 'hang' with a bunch of boring people?" Even worse, the professionals encouraging you to make these changes are just robotically performing their duty. "These people don't really know what to do. They are coming with these ideas because they don't have real answers to my challenges. Maybe my old friends are not the most constructive group. But hell, at least we enjoy each other."

For those of you in this category, here is another way to think about this type of mindset. Let's pretend that you and your new network of friends are "blue food coloring" and that you want to stay blue. You also believe that no matter what anyone says, thinks, or does to you, you are always going to be "blue."

Now, imagine that your current network of less than constructive friends are composed of "yellow food coloring." Your belief is that if you mix with just a little bit of that yellow food coloring with your blue food coloring, you are still going to still stay blue. It won't change that much. You might be a lighter blue. But the fact is, you are going to stay BLUE!

Next, do this experiment: take 10 drops of blue food coloring, put it in water, and mix it. Then, I want you to take one drop of yellow food coloring and put in the water.

So what happens? Does the water become lighter blue? Is there any blue at all? Is there any yellow at all? No! The water actually turns GREEN! It's a completely different color. Now, try to change the water color back to blue by adding blue food coloring drops. How many drops did it take? 10? More than 10? You are going to need a lot of blue food coloring drops to get back to the original color.

So how does this play out in life? If you think that you can simultaneously be with your old "yellow food coloring homies" and remain constructively "blue," it will not happen! You are going to be infected with green. You will be influenced by your old friends not staying true to your genuine color. This is a law of nature. It does not change. Hence, you are going to need to be around a healthy group in order to move forward in your life.

Respectfully consider how you develop your social network. We don't want you to turn "green." We prefer to see you stay in the "royal blue" color status you are trying to achieve.

Humility and Vulnerability

In closing this final chapter, renowned song writer/lyricist, Avicii, sums up the crucial elements of finding mentors and creating a constructive social network in his hit song, "Lay Me Down."

> "Lay Me Down"
> Lay me, La-La Lay me
> La-La Lay me
> La-La Lay me down
> Lay me, La-La Lay me
> La-La Lay me
> La-La, Lay me down
> Lay me, La-La Lay me
> La-La Lay me
> La-La, Lay me down'

I feel weak, things get tough
Sometimes my knees can barely hold me up
I'm no fool, but it's said
You gotta walk a mile 'til you're outta my head

Come within, taste it up
Take a little bit and baby don't you give up
Cast your light, give a damn
You gotta make a move and show me where we can stand
Lay me down in darkness
Tell me what you see
Love is where the heart is
Show me I'm the one, tell me I'm the one that you need
(Come on)
Lay me down in darkness
Tell me what you see
Love is where the heart is
Show me I'm the one, tell me I'm the one that you need
(Come on)

Tell me I'm the one, tell me I'm the one that you need
Tell me I'm the one, tell me I'm the one that you need

[Nile:]
I got the time, it'll be alright, yeah, I got the time
that you need (yeah)

We all weep, bleed the same
If you get the picture, leave it outta the frame
In the now, take a chance
Make a mess, and don't forget that life is a dance

Come within, taste it up
Take a little bit and baby don't you give up
Cast your light, give a damn
You gotta make a move and show me where we can stand

Lay me down in darkness
Tell me what you see
Love is where the heart is
Show me I'm the one, tell me I'm the one that you need
(Come on)

Lay me down in darkness (yeah)
Tell me what you see
Love is where the heart is
Show me I'm the one, tell me I'm the one that you need
(Come on)

[Nile Riff:]
Show me I'm the one tell me I'm the one that you need
(Yeah)
Show me I'm the one tell me I'm the one that you need
Show me I'm the one tell me I'm the one that you need
Show me I'm the one tell me I'm the one that you need

Mmmm-mmm me, show me baby baby tell me that's me, yeah
I got the time, it'll be alright, yeah
I got the time that you need. Come on!

La-la-lay me
La-la-lay me down
La-la-lay me
La-la-lay me down
La-la- lay me
La-la-lay me down
La-la-lay me
La-la-lay me down
Lay me.. in darkness
                              -Avicii

If you like the lyrics, then you are going to really love the song. I suggest checking at:
http://www.youtube.com/watch?v=xFPFEa2VMMA

If it hits home at all, you might consider downloading this song. The energy, vibe, and lyrics accentuate the importance of recognizing our dark blind spots, humbly laying down our need for help, and vulnerably requesting guidance from others.

There is increasing literature demonstrating that great music can help support our temporal lobes. Our temporal lobes are responsible for keeping our anger, frustration, and irritability under control. Hence, a song like "Lay Me Down" can be a great hit tune used to help your brain function at a higher level and remain calm. Be mindful, be humble, and lay your brain down to higher powers that support its higher functioning.

Summary

1. Mentors unconditionally accept others and simultaneously guide them toward greater goals.
2. You are going to need at least one great mentor in your life.
3. Mentors are great tools when we hit obstacles and emotional tension.
4. Many who have become involved with the legal system have been parented with insecure attachments.
5. Don't worry, there is hope. More than 40 percent of the population has been reared with insecure attachments. You are not alone.
6. Mentoring can lead to some constructive emotional discomfort through the process of change.
7. Between mentoring sessions, find a group of constructive friends for support and guidance.
8. Blue + Yellow does not equal light blue. Blue + Yellow = Green. Don't turn green!

Questions

1. Reflecting back, who has been a great mentor in your life? What did they do? What qualities did they demonstrate?
2. If you did not have any mentors, whom do you wish could have been a mentor for you? What qualities did they demonstrate?

3. Substance abuse support meetings are one reasonable place to find a mentor. What other places could you look to find a mentor? What people are involved in your life right now who might be a good mentor?

4. From your past experiences, what words would you use to describe a mentor, both positive and negative (reliable, consistent, honest or sneaky, power hungry, bossy, etc.)? Looking ahead, what would be some ideal qualities that you would look for in a mentor?

5. Socially, there will be lots of encounters with people. How do you figure who is safe versus unsafe? What do safe and unsafe mean to you?

6. If someone is not safe for you to be around, how can you diplomatically handle this situation?

7. If we are a reflection of the five closest people with whom we spend time, then who are those five people in your life? What qualities do they embody? How close are your values aligned to their values?

8. What are your values? If you are not sure, another way to ask the question is of which qualities of life do you place the most focus (family, stability, adventure, adversity, etc.)?

9. How can you find people who hold similar values to your own?

10. What leaders do you trust? Who do you respect? How can you find people of those same qualities to be part of your life?

11. Asking others for help can bring up a number of different emotions. When you truly don't know an answer to something, how do you feel asking someone else for help?

12. When people offer guidance, what are your initial thoughts and feelings? Do you feel like you need to do exactly as they say...or else? Do you internally rebel thinking that your way is much better?

13. How can you learn to discern helpful advice from less instructive counsel?

14. How can you learn to ask good questions about the guidance that has been suggested?

15. If you disagree with someone's recommendations, how can you respectfully and honestly let them know such that you can continue to build a more secure (versus insecure!) attachment for a long-term friendship?

NOTES

EPILOGUE

This book began with a story about Elon Musk and his vision to change the world with the Tesla electronic car. It seems only fitting to finish this book with one last parting tale about the evolutionary source of energy.

As the development of this battery started to take shape, a major concern was its safety. Musk wanted to make sure the large magnitude of the energy unit would not harbor any potential pitfalls. One major hazard would be fires. Any time there is energy produced, there is heat. Where heat is manufactured, there is always the possibility of unexplained combustions.

One only needs to look at what happened on a Boeing 787 Dreamliner plane on a runway in Boston. In January 2013, a sudden unexpected fire broke out from the rechargeable lithium battery. The sudden increase in temperature led to extensive smoke damage to the jet. Fortunately, no one was injured.1

To avoid such disasters, Musk preemptively made some changes to the Tesla battery. Most batteries produced are large, bulky, and quite powerful. If a temperature increase occurs, the battery's sheer mass in size makes it difficult to control its thermal power. The excess in temperature can lead to a "runway" flare up. Once that ignition starts, BOOM! A chain-like reaction occurs that is difficult to stop.

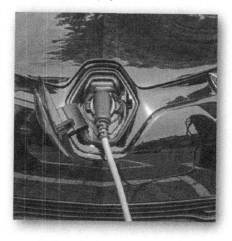

To avert such a disaster, Musk had the engineering team make some changes. Rather than have one oversized massive battery, Musk decided to create small "mini-unit" batteries, connect a large number of them together, and allow their additive power to propel the Tesla.2 A smaller battery unit produces less heat. Should one unit become too hot, it could be shut down before other smaller units would be equally affected. This preemptive move would prevent a subsequent, uncontrollable inferno from happening.

Next, Musk added one additional precautionary measure. Around each simplified cell, a fireproofing "intumescent goo" was sprayed.3 Under heightened temperatures, a chemical reaction occurs within the goo creating a heat repellant foam. This frothy substance covers the over-energized cell, resulting in a reduction in heat. Moreover, the material protects the other small batteries, preventing a domino-like effect that would result in a large out-of-control fire.

Theoretically, Musk knew that such a battery could be made and produced. However, because of the thousands of small batteries that would be connected and sprayed, the overall cost would go up significantly. To make matters even more complex, the engineering team was uncertain if the project would work. Would enough energy be produced to run a car with such small batteries? If so, how far would the car run before it needed a recharge? Would this design really prevent fires?

To this date, there have been no actual fires in any of the cars. Musk's meticulous care focusing on power and safety has been successful. The design's emphasis on precision, small details, microscopic circuitry, and complex synchronicity have resulted in a fast, durable, and safe energy source.

As one reflects on the brilliance of Musk's achievement, it very much reflects what you will need to do to rehabilitate your brain. The thousands of cells in the Tesla battery resemble the numerous skill sets, practice activities, and ideas that are in this book. They may seem mundane, boring, cumbersome, inconvenient, trite, purposeless, trivial, superficial, and unimportant. When each unit is viewed individually, that philosophical belief may very well be true. You will not be able to travel far if only one cell is working effectively.

However, what happens when you get all cells working together in harmony? What happens if we stopped trivializing scheduling and actually make a weekly game plan? What if we discontinue minimizing the importance of self-esteem and genuinely engaged in improving it? What if we could stop rationalizing "just one drink" and intentionally quit consuming alcohol? Moreover, what is the additive (or exponential) power of doing all these activities at once?

What type of cerebral symphony could be created? How much shear raw power would be manufactured? As you intentionally engage in the book's recommendations, it is actually like adding one small "mini-unit" battery to your brain. It may not seem like much of a change. If however, you add enough of these small energy sources over time, your brain begins to harbor the same power as the Tesla engine: a brain that gives back purpose to the world... and a brain that stays out of jail.

After you start adding these energy units, they will need to be sprayed with the "intumescent goo" of protection. That goo is your "bodyguard." It is your new security system. It keeps your brain away from those things that are not so healthy for it. Toxins such as alcohol and drugs can result in unpleasant and explosive consequences. Negative influences can corrode newly developing belief systems resulting in regretful behaviors. A lack of self-awareness may lead to highly charged feelings of anger not being sufficiently cooled.

In closing, this book will hopefully be one of many that you read, understand, and process to develop a healthier brain. Such a brain will make better decisions, live more fully, connect more closely, and prosper more successfully.

As you go on your journey, please let me know how you are doing. That is very important to me. I can be reached at jay@drjayfaber.com or visit my website, www. drjayfaber.com. You can also find me active on Facebook, Instagram, LinkedIn, Twitter, and YouTube. Additional hard copies of the book can be secured on Amazon.com or you can print your own copies at www.drjayfaber.com

Dr. Jay Faber is a double board certified Adult and Child/Adolescent Psychiatrist. He specializes in neuroimaging and holistic care to bring a higher quality of life, mentally and physically, for his patients.

Currently, Dr. Faber practices at the Amen Clinics in Costa Mesa, CA. He is an active member of American Psychiatric Association, The American Academy of Child and Adolescent Psychiatry, and the American Academy of Anti-Aging Medicine.

In addition to Escape, Dr. Faber has also produced, Fortified Friendships, an audio visual media presentation teaching adolescents the vital social skills necessary to be successful in life.

BIBLIOGRAPHY

Preface

1. Elon Musk, Wikipedia. (https://en.wikipedia.org/wiki/Elon_Musk)

2. Pelley, Scott (March 30, 2014). "Tesla and Space-X: Elon Musk's Industrial Empire (http://www.cbsnews.com/news/tesla-and-spacex-elon-musks-industrial-empire/)

3. Tesla Motors Web Page. (https://www.tesla.com/models/design)

4. Pelley, Scott (March 30, 2014). "Tesla and Space-X: Elon Musk's Industrial Empire (http://www.cbsnews.com/news/tesla-and-spacex-elon-musks-industrial-empire/)

Chapter 1

1. R. B. Lopez, W. Hofmann, D. D. Wagner, W. M. Kel- ley, T. F. Heatherton. Neural Predictors of Giving in to Temptation in Daily Life. Psychological Science, 2014

Chapter 2

1. http://business.time.com/2013/11/15/candy-crush-saga-the-science-behind-our-addiction/

2. Nathaniel Brandon; "The Power of Self-Esteem"

3. Nathaniel Brandon; "The Power of Self-Esteem"

4. Robert Greene; "Mastery"

5. Brandon Burchard; "The Charge"

6. Rick Warren; "The Purpose Driven Life"

Chapter 3

1. http://www.cnn.com/2014/02/28/showbiz/philip-seymour-hoffman-autopsy/index.html

2. The National Center on Addiction and Substance Abuse at Columbia University; Behind Bars II: Substance Abuse and America's Prison Population, February 2010

3. Bahr, SJ et al; Successful Reentry: What Differentiates Successful and Unsuccessful Parolees?; epub. 2009 Jul 28

4. https://www.centeronaddiction.org/addiction-research/reports/behind-bars-ii-substance-abuse-and-america%E2%80%99s-prison-population

5. Ferguson et al; J. Head Trauma Rehabilitation; Vol. 27, No.

6. Amen DG, Yantis S, Trudeau J, Stubblefield MS, Halverstadt JS. "Visualizing the Firestorms in the Brain: An Inside Look at the Clinical and Physiological Connections between Drugs and Violence Using Brain SPECT Imaging," Journal of Psychoactive Drugs, Vol. 29 (4), 1997, 307-319.

7. Amen DG, Hanks C, Prunella, JR, Green, "An Analysis of Regional Cerebral Blood Flow in Impulsive Murderers Using Single Photon Emission Computed Tomography." J Neuropsychiatry Clin Neurosci 2007 Summer; 19(3): 304-9.

Chapter 4

1. Steve Farber; "Greater Than Yourself"

2. Marin, RS and Gorovoy IR, : "Echothymia: Environmental Dependency in the Affective Domain". Jour. of Neuropsych. and Neuroclin. Sc.; 2014; 26:92-96.com and http://www.societyforunderstanding.co.uk

3. Paul Hannam and John Selby; "Take Charge of Your Mind"

Chapter 5

1. https://youthbuild.org/graduate-page/hall-achievement

2. Sharon L. Lechter and Greg S. Reid; "Three Feet From Gold"

Epilogue

1. Pelley, Scott (March 30, 2014). "Tesla and Space-X: Elon Musk's Industrial Empire (http://www.cbsnews.com/news/tesla-and-spacex-elon-musks-industrial-empire/)

2. Pelley, Scott (March 30, 2014). "Tesla and Space-X: Elon Musk's Industrial Empire (http://www.cbsnews.com/news/tesla-and-spacex-elon-musks-industrial-empire/)

3. Pelley, Scott (March 30, 2014). "Tesla and Space-X: Elon Musk's Industrial Empire (http://www.cbsnews.com/news/tesla-and-spacex-elon-musks-industrial-empire/)

Made in the USA
Las Vegas, NV
07 March 2024

86827868R00066